a place

WISCONSIN WRITERS

to which

ON WISCONSIN LANDSCAPES

we belong

EDITED BY DENNIS BOYER & JUSTIN ISHERWOOD

foreword by gaylord nelson

Published in 1998 by
The 1000 Friends of Wisconsin Land Use Institute
16 N. Carroll St, Suite 810
Madison, WI 53703

Illustrations: Owen Coyle
Cover photo: Dave Cieslewicz
Cover design: Nancy Zucker

Printed in the United States of America

ISBN 0-966659-0-6

This book is dedicated to
Walter Kuhlmann and Kristin Visser.
Two Wisconsin conservationists who left us
with so much, but left us so early.

Contents

PART THREE   SPIRITS

Foreword

SENATOR GAYLORD NELSON

The title of this anthology is an adaptation of a famous quote from Aldo Leopold:

> *"We abuse land because we regard it as a commodity belonging to us. When we see land as a community to which we belong, we may begin to use it with love and respect."*

The purpose of these essays is to get the reader thinking about his community — the place to which he belongs — so that we can get to work on the transformation in our thinking that Leopold believed was a prerequisite for progress.

This anthology presents a range of Wisconsin voices — past and present — on the irresistible pull of the Wisconsin landscape. The contributors give us insights about how we shape the land and how it shapes us. They help us answer the twin questions of what is Wisconsin and what it means to be a Wisconsinite.

For example, my old friend Bud Jordahl writes touchingly about his family's three-decade long work of restoring an old farm in Richland County. The hard physical labor of healing the land is paying benefits in abundant wildlife. Now, Bud is turning his attention to assuring that his land will always be well cared for, even if ownership changes hands. His story captures both the beauty of the region that drew him and the interaction with the land that shaped his attitudes and ideas.

I am also pleased to see an essay by the late George Vukelich. "The Blue Canoe" is among his best work and we're indebted to George's family for allowing the use of his essay in this anthology.

Most often, collections of outdoor writing focus only on rural places. This anthology is different because it contains several wonderful pieces about urban settings. Marc Eisen's description of ice skating with his children in his Madison neighborhood serves as a fine reminder of the pleasures of city life.

i

This book celebrates the gentle, beautiful subtlety of the Wisconsin landscape and the solid character of its settlements as it challenges us to protect them. Will Fantle carries on the tradition of Rachel Carlson as he explores the causes of the deformed amphibians showing up in his Eau Claire neighborhood. Paul Hayes, who was for many years the Milwaukee Journal's fine environmental writer, recounts the changes that have come and which are coming to his beloved Cedar Creek.

A look at these essays and excerpts will convince the reader that the diversity of nature finds full expression in the hearts of those who write about the Wisconsin they love. Favorite marshes, beloved lakes, remembered homesteads, and treasured outdoor moments inhabit these pages. Political attitudes, social critiques, ecological values, historical perspective and spiritual growth wind their way in and out of our writers' words.

These essays remind us that Wisconsin is not one story. It is many stories. Stories about a place to which we belong.

Gaylord Nelson
Washington, D.C.
September 1998

Introduction

Which sentiments shape our relationship with the landscape? Which lenses, prisms and filters magnify, bend and clarify our view of our special piece of the Earth?

Such questions have been around for a long time in Wisconsin. We debate, philosophize and, on occasion, trade shots over them.

It was ever thus. Prehistory's struggles over hunting grounds gave way to French and British fur wars and finally the United States grid of plat sections meant to organize the land for homesteaders. Put names and voices to the Wisconsin angle: Black Hawk and One-Eyed Decorah on one end, Muir and Leopold in the middle, and Gaylord Nelson and dozens of citizen action groups planted in the here and now.

When 1000 Friends of Wisconsin put out the call for essays, there was perhaps a fuzzy idea that we would elicit the bounty of pastoral warmth which generally characterizes the "outdoors piece." We saw those, to be sure, many crafted by Wisconsin's best wordsmiths. But there were surprises in the daily mailbag too.

It turned out that when you ask folks for their personal angle on the human sense of place, a wide variety of things pop into their heads. Some of it cranky and some of it arcane.

Perhaps this is to be expected from a group as diverse as our contributors. Grab some journalists and outdoor writers, season with academics and activists, and serve up garnished with those who wield their pens for novels, church bulletins, and poetry collections.

It was our aim to keep our hands off the message and simply find ways to make the collection fit within space and cost parameters. We hope our contributors feel that our editorial touch was sufficiently light. If not, apologies are in order and 1000 Friends of Wisconsin will dock our pay accordingly.

Our deepest thanks go out to those contributors. Not only for their time and effort, but for the openness and intimacy of their sharing. May we all hoist mugs together!

Editorial collaboration and partnership is a tricky task for grouchy middle-aged guys such as we. Especially when there are chores at home, fish to be caught, and rivers to be canoed. The bond of homebrews, microbrews, and tavern tales filled the assignment with chuckles, grins, and warm correspondence.

Thanks are in order to all who made this anthology possible: Steve Salemson, Patty Mayers, Jerry Minnich, Miriam Brown, Nancy Zucker, and Owen Coyle. The diligent staff of 1000 Friends of Wisconsin kept the project moving ahead while the coeditors insisted on cooking their brains in the summer sun: hats off! Special thanks to Andrea Dearlove for the final cleanup editing. Loyal spouses Lynn and Donna put up with our diversion, assisted more than they anticipated, and thus watched our debt grow from a fish fry dinner to a prime rib with all the trimmings.

Justin Isherwood
Plover

Dennis Boyer
Linden

people and place

Arwain Fi I Graig Afyddo Uwch Nami

Psalm 61 from the Gaelic, "lead me to a rock higher than i"

JUSTIN ISHERWOOD

A crescent smile lies across the belly of Wisconsin, a geological province called the Central Plain. Stranded in this region of remarkable flatness are mesas and buttes whose formation is owed to a patient Cambrian time and its warm sea. What is extraordinary about these sandstone outliers is their next geological abundance is far to the west in Montana, Utah and Colorado's Monument Valley. These buttes and mesas were born beneath the sea whose shallows were moved by the wind. A desolate planet whose atmosphere was yet toxic, quite at home with that hostile gang of Venus and Mars, a place untried by green plants.

The mesas of central Wisconsin go by names both strange and familiar: Roche a'Cri, Friendship Mound, Petenwell, Ship Rock and Liberty Bluff. Like sacked castles they rise over some of the dab flattest land in North America, the sort an unambitious and languid sea might contrive.

Below the village of Bancroft stands the last butte, north is the Buena Vista Marsh and just beyond, the rim of the Northern Highland, a geological province where granite does the underwriting, not sand. The last butte is known among locals by a variety of names: the Ledge, Indian Rock, Gullliver's Stool and somehow always as Lover's Leap. And yes, there is a local legend of Indian lovers who either ought not or could not, and from the summit of that rock took up their Shakespearean revenge.

I have long known of the Ledge, since a child I pedaled on a fat-tire Schwinn down the sandy road crossing the marsh — I had heard from my grandmother of "an carraig" and as a kid I prospected for it, feeling grand as Edmund Hillary with my expedition. The Ledge was my horizon, squatting its huddled shape beyond the south face, blemishing what was otherwise empirically flat. A great hoary aunt lived on a tangled dirt lane in the shadow of the carraig and it was family custom to visit her once or twice in the summer. Clayton, the son of this great gar, farmed as a man might under the spell of this time-jealous butte. He plowed yet with the crusade beasts of River Clyde; I think my father visited for that. My dad had gone tractor and in the repentance of those sins to McCormick and John Deere, wished on the sabbath to smell horsepower in the flesh. To smell again the saddle soap and lanolin of Clayton's tack room, and smell, if you can believe it, a horse-drawn bottom spilling God's own sweet furrow.

Cousin Clayton and great great lived in that certain departure from social convention as is custom among the keepers, those known to be the family keepers, or what passed for genealogy in that time. The parlor of the farmhouse appeared unchanged in the last millennium, ovals of ancestors were ranked on the walls; grim, unsmiling ancestors whose eyes seemed to hungrily follow me. I thought their gaze hinted of predation. My grandma and the great great ruin spoke in hushed tones beneath the convening molder of those attentive oval fossils.

I could not have been induced to visit Uncle Clayton's farm, it being more a mausoleum than a farmhouse, had it not been for the kitchen. As searing white as the front parlor was dark and sarcophic. Windows were everywhere, white walls, white cupboards, a white porcelain gas stove, a wide and also white kitchen sink, frig (they were all white then), and over the front door hung Clayton's varmint gun. Every farmhouse kitchen once required by a force higher than the town assessor to have a varmint gun hung over the door. Uncle Clayton's was a rolling block twenty-two whose gray barrel and weathered stock spoke of rabbit hunting while shucking corn. The rifle, hanging from a nail on the wagon box, made the day spent at slave labor somehow worthwhile.

Was Clayton who spoke of the ledge. "You come down on a Sunday afternoon and I'll take you." Following the consistent pattern of over-abundant farm chores he died before he could lead me there. But the ruin of a carraig persisted and on a Sunday afternoon in the spring of 1956 I rode my hot rod Schwinn across the marsh to find that rock. It does not take a genius to find a high thing. It was there all right, below the village on the far side of the railroad tracks. Pried out of flat ground in a most sur-real fashion, a pedestal of stratified vengeance that had stood in the self-same spot for half a billion years. The west slope given over to scrub oak and arbutus, higher up, rooted in the crags were contorted white pine, caught in the act of sucking their nourishment. Looking at that rock made a poet of a farm kid, seeing in the rock ripples of a sea wind told a time before, before Adam, before dinosaurs, if not even before God.

I was ten, lean and slightly translucent and it took awhile looking at that rune stone to find courage enough to climb it. Because everything in me, everything in my ancestors, even in the ancestors of my ancestors, was

2

eclipsed by that rock. The modern year of 1956 wasn't anything to it. Neither was A.D., B.C., Adolf Hitler, Babe Ruth, Jesus Christ nor Hank Aaron coming to bat bottom of the ninth with two men on.

I learned on that day what it means to be absorbed and rendered infinitesimal by a place, and how this feeling, as unbecoming as it is to our species, is worth the insult. This desire for old rocks, old trees, old rivers; for experienced places, worn places, shadowed places; this impulse for museums, old books, old words, old nature; and resulting in a terrible sensation that comes to a person caught in the riptide of half a billion years. The horizon falls away, our thoughts are less of humankind than of angels hovering above the insincere planet, and quite to our own surprise enjoying the spectacle, never mind the plot includes their mortal remains.

I still climb the rock, though Uncle Clayton is long gone, as is his house and horses; a center pivot irrigation runs over what used to be his front yard. I took the girl who was to become my wife to that rock. I knew I had chosen well when she skinned her knee gaining the top but fell immediately into a stillness by which I knew her worth, and had as a consequence the rock's consent. I carried my children up to the topmost edge overlooking the sand plain, as baptized there as in the little white kirk at the junction of county roads. My mother has since confessed to me that her Raymond took her to the rock before they were married, how she never liked heights but he pulled her up anyway and they were joined by a force older than Moses.

The best time is in the morning when the tumbler of dawn is yet empty and only a little smudged by yesterday's lips. To climb out of the shadow of night to meet halfway up the first leaking light of day, the kit bag slapping on your hip, a thermos of oolong and a china cup. Below and all around is the peneplain of the Great Alluvial, the sun preens on the moraine like a morning bird. On this rippled rock, know what climbers know, that scale against which we are invisible, but another sea-change, a ripple at best. Season and millennia fall away and it is the stone who is consciousness.

We are wise to keep nature close, to fence off places that our selfish opulence can so easily overwhelm. To keep places, simple places where a child on a fat-tired bike can sit on the floor of a vanquished sea watching a disinterested star pull loose from the hills. We can not transistorize, we can not e-mail, poly-wrap or reduce to a serum ... the holy.

Justin Isherwood is author of the Book of Plough *and farms near Plover.*

Early Voyage

FATHER MARQUETTE

We knew that, at three leagues from Maskoutens, was a river which discharged into Missisipi. We knew also that the direction we were to follow in order to reach it was west-southwesterly. But the road is broken by so many swamps and small lakes that it is easy to lose one's way, especially as the river leading thither is so full of wild oats that it is difficult to find the channel. For this reason we greatly needed our two guides, who safely conducted us to a portage of 2,700 paces, and helped us to transport our canoes to enter that river; after which they returned home, leaving us alone in this unknown country, in the hands of Providence [at the site of Portage, Wisconsin].

Thus we left the waters flowing to Quebeq, four or five hundred leagues from here, to float on those that would thenceforward take us through strange lands. Before embarking thereon, we began all together a new devotion to the blessed Virgin Immaculate, which we practised daily, addressing to her special prayers to place under her protection both our persons and the success of our voyage; and, after mutually encouraging one another, we entered our canoes.

The river on which we embarked is called Meskousing [Wisconsin]. It is very wide; it has a sandy bottom, which forms various shoals that render its navigation very difficult. It is full of islands covered with vines. On the banks one sees fertile land, diversified with woods, prairies, and hills. There are oak, walnut, and basswood trees; and another kind, whose branches are armed with long thorns. We saw there neither feathered game nor fish, but many deer, and a large number of cattle.

After proceeding 40 leagues on this same route, we arrived at the mouth of our river; and, at 42 and a half degrees of latitude, we safely entered Missisipi on the 17th of June, with a joy that I cannot express.

Father Marquette's diary is the earliest European-American account of Wisconsin features.

Wisconsin

BILL STOKES

Wisconsin had a big party in 1998. It was a roll-out-the-barrel, slice-the-cheese, strike-up-the-polka-band wing-ding that promised to roust every last badger out of state burrows and into the streets to dance with guests.

On May 29, Wisconsin was officially 150 years old, which is not old for its rocks and rivers, but is old for its trees and trails. For the state, itself, however, it is just right. Prime, you might say. Like a three-year-old cow called Bucolic, or a 28-year-old quarterback called Brett, or properly aged cheese called Brick.

Now you don't celebrate such a significant birthday on just one day. That would be like blowing out only one of the birthday candles. Instead you set up committees and commissions, and you make more plans than the mother of the bride.

And so it came to pass: from Cornucopia to Kenosha and La Crosse to Sheboygan, some part of the party was going on almost everyday of 1998.

"We wanted to involve everyone," said Governor Tommy Thompson, who jumped on his Milwaukee-made Harley and rode to Washington, D.C. to invite the entire country.

Virtually every community had some special event, and there were so many reunions that if you didn't have a rich, long-lost uncle you could probably find one by dropping in on someone else's get-together.

It was a bash, and if there were Wisconsin residents who did not want to join in, they headed for the hills, of which there are many.

Not to put a party-pooper spin on things, but there are actually a few people in the state who say that although celebrations are fine, they like Wisconsin for its peace and quiet, and please turn down the music a little and don't slam the door when you leave.

They are the same people who think that wearing "Green Bay Packer" underwear is excessive. They do, however, have a point: Wisconsin's character, for those who live there and for those who are drawn to visit, may be defined as somewhat doe-eyed and buck-solitary. We Badgers may love our beer and brats, but we also demand a certain amount of down time, which means that we love the thousands of places where the only sound is the wind in the trees or the gentle lap of blue water on a birch-rimmed lake shore.

Those of us who have spent most of our lives in Wisconsin have a special feeling for it, and we understand how people who live in the metro-mazes and the soybean deserts like to come and visit. We welcome them, of course, and we especially welcomed them in 1998. And if we cannot communicate our special feeling for our state, it is probably because we don't quite understand it ourselves.

My own sense of Wisconsin is rooted, literally, on a small dairy farm in the northwestern part of the state, where cows stood more or less in the shadow of the big North Woods. My boyhood was like the growing season for a stalk of corn — close to the earth and the elements; and on rainy days I could feel the State of Wisconsin squishing up between my bare toes. Somehow, that kind of experience encourages the perception that although you may be different from the stalk of corn, some of that is only in your mind.

There were remnants of huge old pine stumps in the pasture where I went to "get the cows" for the twice-daily milking, and they were like the splinters of family and community history that you could pick up to feel and smell. A gnarled old Norwegian grandfather talked about the days when the big trees were sawed down and floated away by a combination of rich eastern opportunists and dirt-poor reckless lumberjacks. It was only much later, obviously, that you could regret that your predecessors belonged to the latter group. For a farm boy growing up on the sprawling grave of the big woods, Grandpa's best story was about the panther high up in the limbs of a giant shadowy white pine, its tail hanging down "like a big fishhook."

Those are the kinds of natural Wisconsin "hooks" that go deep. And although it may be possible to live in Wisconsin and not have an appreciation of the natural scheme of things, it seems unlikely. Aldo Leopold finally put some of that down in his little book called "A Sand County Almanac." It talks about natural harmony, which many Wisconsin people may not know by name, but which they inherently use to style their lives.

The lifestyle of a real badger is rodent-like, of course. They are among the largest members of the weasel family, they live in burrows and they smell bad. And because they are relatively sparsely distributed and nocturnal, few Wisconsin residents have ever seen one. ("Bucky Badger," the University of Wisconsin mascot is obviously an exception to all of the above.)

As every Wisconsin school child knows, Wisconsin residents call themselves "badgers" because of the first white settlers who dug burrows to mine lead down in the southwestern corner of the state, thereby acting —

but certainly not smelling, more or less like real badgers.

And, as the school kids also know, before the arrival of those first human Badgers, the area that became Wisconsin had a long history of Native Americans. They lived in hundreds of places along the rivers and lakes, and their earliest records are written in the stone tools they left behind and in some of the caves they used for shelter.

In one of those caves recently, an anthropologist found the remnants of rare rock painting dating back thousands of years. Within months, someone sneaked in and used a stone saw to try to remove the paintings, apparently to sell them. The attempt failed, but it did incalculable damage to the art work. That angered a lot of Wisconsin people who value not only the history of their own people but of the Native Americans' as well.

The history of the relationship of the Native Americans and the rest of the Wisconsin citizens is now being written in the 17 casinos that the tribes operate across the state. If you drive from Madison, where I live, to the Ho Chunk casino near Wisconsin Dells, you pass the historical markers that describe the massacre of Chief Black Hawk's people as they fled across Wisconsin from Illinois in 1882. It was a shameful episode, and if you think about it at a blackjack table you will probably lose your concentration and go "bust."

There was great consternation several years ago when some of the Native Americans exercised treaty rights that allowed them to spear walleyes. Walleyes are almost sacred to some Wisconsin residents, among them the operators of northern resorts. The walleye issue has settled down somewhat, but like the casino issue, it is fraught with politics and emotion, and of great concern to the state's tourist industry.

As important as tourism is to Wisconsin's economy, it is a mixed bag for the citizenry. In fact, there are those who view it as a curse, and an infringement on their God-given Badger rights to tranquillity. On the highways, for example, the acronym for the frequent expression of this sentiment is GDID. The last two words are "Illinois Driver" and the first two are a blasphemy.

The situation cuts both ways, of course, and big-city drivers — conditioned as they are to competing for the victory lap — are not taken too seriously by Wisconsin drivers if they over-react to a load of hay or a manure spreader holding up traffic on the road to the "best Friday night fish fry," or the loudest roadhouse rock music.

The value of time is viewed with a certain democracy in Wisconsin: You are going there, and I'm going here, and who is to say that your mission is more important than mine? Some of this harks back to the days when it was common to see official traffic signs that read, "Cattle Crossing."

Now what you commonly see are signs that say, "Deer Crossing." These signs display a leaping buck deer, and so far, nobody, not even the Madison feminists, has complained about this roadside sexism. People in Wisconsin love deer. They drive country roads on spring or autumn evenings to admire them, and then they also use bows and arrows and guns to kill about a half a million of them every fall. Deer are a crop, like the cute little baby chicks that end up as Sunday chicken dinners.

And as all Wisconsin residents and visitors know, killing deer is not confined to woods and weapons. It occurs daily on the roads when deer fail to concede that drivers have the right-of-way. Some 40,000 to 50,000 deer are killed each year in traffic accidents.

But that conjures up an unjustly bloody image for a state of shy creatures and gentle people. What you have in Wisconsin is a kind of straight ahead pragmatism that acknowledges that if you are going to eat a hamburger, somebody has to kill a cow. In today's society, that fact is increasingly obscured by a city and suburban population that does not recognize that "hunting and gathering" goes beyond the supermarket. Perhaps in some subtle ways, living in Wisconsin or even visiting it, serves to correct that. You cannot drive the rolling green hills or the winding wooded roads and not be constantly reminded of "nature," and of its all-encompassing character and therefore its inevitable embrace. There is therapy in that.

More common knowledge is that much of Wisconsin was appropriately designed by a glacier some 10,000 years ago, and each winter there are periods of weather that cause residents to suspect that the glacier is returning. It may be, but in the meantime winter is really the king season in the state, and people survive it with a blend of brawn, bravado and appreciation for snow-decked beauty. Of course, a little brandy also helps.

Liquid stimulants — brandy and beer, for example — may be part of the Wisconsin fabric, but what really defines our state is water. Except for the border it shares with Illinois, Wisconsin abuts water, and its interior is dotted and laced with so many lakes and rivers that if it were a boat it would sink. All of this is the work of the Wisconsin glacier, and although it deemed water as kind, it also set a watery and wooded stage on which the seasonal progression is as colorful and dramatic as the circus show in Baraboo.

Spring in Wisconsin comes tiptoeing up the river valleys in a pale green prom dress, flinging plum blossom corsages at the hills and yodeling like a sandhill crane. It is usually late, but worth the wait, and then it matures into a summer that is so lush and green you would think the cows might give green milk. These summers are often hot and humid, punctuated by booming thunderstorms and overlain with days of brilliant sunshine. They sizzle like that for a couple of months — until the last Badger has finally taken off his winter underwear — and then they explode into autumn brilliance that takes your breath away, especially in places where yellow birch and red maple rim the blue water. Then it is winter's turn again.

So as this cycle occurred in 1998, Wisconsin celebrated its 150th birthday. The party reached a crescendo during the summer when mosquitoes presided over thousands of ritualistic blood-lettings and ants held court on the picnic tables. This is what some of the party-goers did: Drove to Door County and let Lake Michigan kiss their cheeks. Put on light jackets and went to Cornucopia to watch a sunset across Lake Superior. Wallowed in the big North Woods and listened for the whispers of lumberjack ghosts. Rode down rivers in canoes and rafts. Spent an afternoon fishing for bluegills. Went to reunions and listened to one more of Uncle Louie's war stories. Ate brats. Drank beer. Ate apple pie at church socials. Hiked trails, especially the Ice Age Trail where the glacier left behind its richest treasure of moraines and lakes.

And so perhaps this epistle has degenerated into something the Tourism Bureau might put out. That cannot be helped. When you spend a lifetime in Wisconsin, your blatant boosterism must be excused.

It is noteworthy that because of the success of its football team, Wisconsin has become nationally known as the land of cheeseheads. We can handle that. We've been called worse; and we are confident that we can hold our own with any of the city slickers. History shows that we always have, and even when Chicago had its big fire, we had a bigger one up in Peshtigo. Some 1,500 casualties instead of a measly 300 or so for Chicago.

I celebrated Wisconsin's birthday summer by doing what I usually do — meandering up and down the trout streams — my family calls it "floundering" — and while I didn't catch tons of trout, I had a great time and so did the mosquitoes. Some people might not enjoy a birthday party where little droplets of your blood are carried off into the brush by tiny insects. But I figure, hey, this is Wisconsin, it gets into your blood one way or another.

Bill Stokes has written many books, essays, and articles about the people and places of Wisconsin. He is the author of Hi-Ho Silver Anyway *and* The River is Us.

9

Rock Island

HOWARD MEAD

On the map, Rock Island is a remote chip of land off the tip of Door County, out beyond Washington Island, heavily forested, bordered by towering limestone cliffs rising from Lake Michigan on the north and west and a sweeping sand beach along the south shore. Rock Island is Wisconsin's most remote state park — a place of peace and solitude.

Once, from the long crescent of beach, my family and I watched a towering thunderhead drift toward us, a sinister cauliflower cloud rumbling deep inside. More clouds blossomed, swelling like giant hot-air balloons, and flashes of lightning darted back and forth between them. When the sound of thunder became one continuous roar, we dashed for our tent tucked behind the sand dune above the beach. And just in time. The storm ripped open with a blinding flash and a jarring crack. In a house, we scarcely would have noticed. Alone on Rock Island, separated from the storm's fury by only thin fabric, we felt very involved. But the onslaught was brief and as the sound of thunder retreated, we emerged to watch the storm's black and purple back move across the lake, trailing softly falling rain.

I have always felt a potent sense of isolation on this island, of being unprotected and close to the natural world. If a gale blows up, you can't climb into your car and drive to a motel. You are stranded, no longer in control. Here, time is suspended. Schedules are switched off, the pace slowed and slowed again.

All the familiar noises—traffic and telephones and radios—abruptly vanish. In their place come elemental sounds—the rhythm of waves brushing across the sand, or of heavy surf pounding against the limestone ledges. Overhead herring gulls cry and along sun dappled woodland trails a white-throated sparrow whistles dreamily.

It is a good day's work to explore the island's perimeter, combing the rocky cobble beaches, watching for the shadows of great fish moving through the clear water and wondering about the ocean-going freighters streaming down the lake. After supper, sometimes, we'd walk around the point of land that separates the wild side of Rock Island from remnants of Chester Thordarson's baronial estate. Sitting on the concrete dock alongside his huge stone boathouse and "Icelandic" great hall, watching the sun slip silently out of sight, we'd wonder about the man who built this incongruous monument. This genius inventor and iron-willed millionaire tried to tame this wild island and build his romantic notion of an Icelandic village. Today, most of what he built is gone, but the deer, the "nuisances" he tried to "exterminate" because they ate his exotic plantings, are still here.

The nights are magic. Lying on the warm sand, stargazing, we marvel at the Milky Way, a brilliant arc spanning the entire sky. We awoke one morning, after such a night, in a vaporous soup. Cut off entirely from the rest of the world, we paced the beach, not wanting to venture into the woods, even on a well-marked trail, in fog so thick. As we walked, I told the children tales of all the travelers who, through time beyond memory, had pulled their fragile bark canoes up on this beach, built their fires and waited out the great storms, or waited, like us, for the fog to lift. Of Indians who had camped here summers to fish with spear and hook and line, and of explorers who passed this way searching for the Northwest Passage that they hoped would lead them to the riches of the Orient. And I told of black-robed missionaries and of the tough little French-Canadian voyageurs, able to portage immense loads and paddle tremendous distances, singing as they went.

We walked along the same beach, canoed close to where they had camped. And it seemed as though nothing had changed. A mystical moment, the fog gray and dense, dampening all sound except the swish of the waves on the sand, a sound so similar to canoe paddle strokes that I felt an urge to shout, "Bonjour, Messieurs" into the mysterious murk. And so, half expecting an answer, I did.

Howard Mead is the former editor and publisher of Wisconsin Trails *magazine.*

A Small Garden

JERRY MINNICH

I was ten years old when I discovered the sanctuaries of reading and gardens. The discoveries were simultaneous. Writing came later.

This was in Allentown, Pennsylvania, a blue-collar town in the heart of the blue-collar Lehigh Valley (Bethlehem Steel, et al), and we were a blue-collar family, although my mother disapproved of the designation and fought against it, and against my father, with all the stubbornness of her Welsh heritage. We were not exactly a Leave-It-to-Beaver family.

The Allentown Public Library was located smack in the heart of downtown, a few doors from the city's busiest intersection, and I was required, in the Indian summer of my fifth-grade year, to search out something or other at the library. It was my first visit.

In the library, it was only moments before I became distracted and forgot completely about the school assignment. I wandered into the children's fiction section and plucked out a slim volume about a boy who was transported, by dreams or magic of some kind, to other lands in other times. Somehow, this appealed to me.

This library had a side door that led to a tiny garden behind the building. It was an old garden, with mature plantings, and so, despite its small size, it was thickly enclosed in greenery. There was a picnic table and one bench, and a round, child-size table and three stools, cast and painted to look like spotted mushrooms, red and white. It was in this garden, lying on the soft, warm grass, that I began to read the book, whose title I cannot remember.

In everyone's life there are defining moments, experiences that function as turning points, for good or for bad. This was a turning point for me. And a good one, occurring on this postage-stamp-size piece of urban land.

I returned often to the library garden that autumn, and even more often the following summer, to lie on the grass or sit at the picnic bench and read. Or even not to read. Since the library was only four blocks from my home, I could visit often, and I did just that. On every visit, the soft green walls enveloped me, muffling not only the traffic on the street outside, but other matters, as well.

As I continued through childhood and into the teen years, I continued to experience gardens as sanctuaries. Oh, sure, there was my father's vegetable and flower garden, but my time spent there was mostly in work, digging out lamb's-quarters and purslane and dandelions, and tapping Japanese beetles into a jar of kerosene. But I sought out other gardens, richly green and private places that became almost mystical to me. When I was twelve, my first bike allowed me to range more widely through town, and it was then that I discovered a secret island garden in a city park, this park quite large. I had to slip through some thick shrubs and through a curtain of trailing willow branches, then wade ten feet through shallow water to reach the island, which was just large enough to hold two large weeping willows, each with slender branches that fell fountain-like to the ground. Secured within the embrace of the willow branches, I knew that this was the very definition of a sanctuary. And I never met anyone else on the island. It was mine.

Gardens are many things to many people. But I believe that sanctuary might be the most treasured gift that any garden provides. I had the privilege recently of visiting the gardens at Versailles, and although I was ambivalent about this study in excess — at once beautiful and obscene — even those grand gardens must have offered sanctuary of a sort to Louis, after he had spent months in the madness of the royal palace in Paris. It's a matter of principle, not of scale.

A garden also acts as a bridge between mankind and wilderness. It is a benign green space that we create for ourselves, either singlely or as a community, to answer some deep need for softening life's sharp edges. I certainly can appreciate John Muir's love of total wildness — I can fairly picture him scrambling in the night down a rocky mountainside, exalting in a thunderstorm, all of God's creation exploding around him — but when the need for solace appears, a quiet green garden is there to answer.

A garden affirms our chosen place in the natural order. We are the only species, after all, that can appreciably influence its environment. And whether this influence is good or bad (and doubtless it is usually and mostly bad) the fact remains that we have this power and we exercise it daily and inexorably. It is not a question of whether we want to change the environment; it is a matter of how. Even pure conservationists have come to believe that active management is necessary to environmental preservation. A garden, then — whether it be large and public or small and private — is one reflection of our chosen relationship to the world around us. This considered relationship is a power we have, unique to our species, it cannot be denied. And how we exercise it tells much about who we are, and what kind of world we will leave to future generations.

A garden also represents our accommodation with the natural world.

When we choose to be the gardener, we make a deal with nature: we will abide by certain rules in growing plants, and the plants will accede to our shaping them somewhat to our needs and pleasures. We will supply water, loamy soil, a modicum of nutrients, and moderate temperatures, and the impatiens will bloom brightly from May to October. When we hike through the Chequamegon National Forest, we admit to being on foreign turf. When a weeping fig is growing in a pot by the living room window, it is on our turf. But the outdoor garden is a meeting place, where bargains are silently made and kept.

I have kept many gardens in my life, none of them expertly, but all of them with a never-ending sense of wonder and appreciation of the life force that is everywhere in every garden. Today I have a small, urban backyard garden full of flowers and ornamental shrubs. Among the roses, the hollies, the alpine currants, the climbing clematis and bittersweet, I still feel that wonder. And sometimes, when I take a book out to the back deck overlooking the little garden, I feel just as warm, dreamy, and safe as I did more than a half-century ago, lying on the grass behind the Allentown Public Library.

Some things never change.

Jerry Minnich is publisher of Prairie Oak Press and author of many Wisconsin guidebooks.

A Little Lake for Little People

LOWELL KLESSIG

The Tomorrow River borders our farm and it is important to adult trout anglers. Little Lake is a tiny, unnamed spring pond impoundment near the Tomorrow. Little Lake is important to little people — little people like Lance and Lukas (our sons), their cousins, their classmates, and their friends.

Walking on Ice — Lance (Age 1)

I asked him if he wanted to go ice fishing. He probably didn't understand the concept but he understood that he would get to go outside with Daddy. There was no hesitation as he mumbled "ya" and shook his head assertively up and down. Chris was worried about the thin December ice and implored me to tether him but she was also relieved to have one less baby in the house.

I packed him in his sled and gave him a little ice cream bucket for his catch. With two poles we ventured forth on the fresh snow. A pileated woodpecker greeted us from the tall pines on the western shore. Lance loved the beat and tapped his pole on the water in the hole.

Breaking the Record — Lance (Age 3), Lukas (Age 2)

Lance was a Little Lake veteran in his third season on the ice when he led his uncle, older cousins, and baby brother to a very unusual experience. He had taken his dad ice fishing on November 14 and was back with more relatives one day later to show off the fish bowl gleaming in the cold sunshine and surrounded by green white pine, white birch and brown, leaf-covered oak. Neither my even more avid ice-angling brother, Dewey, nor I had ever been ice fishing that early in the season. We doubted our sons would ever break the record they set with us.

The Zero Troop — Lance (Age 5), Lukas (Age 4)

I considered calling off the outing because the temperature was below zero. But on the last of the holiday break before school resumed, I didn't have the heart to break four young hearts — especially since two of them had no father to take them to some special lake.

Their mother delivered them all bundled up in snowsuits, boots, and mittens. I'm sure she was more than a little bit apprehensive about sending her babies out in harsh weather with an uncertified troop leader known to be more fanatic about ice fishing than most men are about holiday football games.

Little Lake was especially serene on that cold, clear, still morning. The northwest shoreline was illuminated by the low hanging, morning sun in the southeast; the rest of the lake lay in the shadows of the trees on the hills that surrounded the lake. The shadows painted the snow a two-tone white along a moving, jagged boundary.

Led by Lance, the boys charged out to the bluegill hole near the center. Usually he helped carry the gear, but with his buddy Jeremy along, that sense of responsibility was completely overwhelmed by the sense of leadership.

I chopped five holes in the futile hope that I might actually get to fish myself. I never did get a fifth line in the water. Lukas caught the first fish — a bluegill. Lance followed suit with five quick ones — Jordan and Jeremy were still trying to get the knack of jigging the pole just a little to make the worm look alive.

A sneaky little fish got Jeremy's worm before he knew he had a bite. I rebaited it. Then Jordan got his cork caught on the ice and had to be reset. Then Lukas needed the slush cleaned out of his hole. Then Lance needed a new worm. Then Jeremy's line got tangled up. Then Jordan's line iced up and wouldn't go down the hole. Then everybody but Lukas wanted a new hole further west. I chopped some more holes with the ice chisel I made in high school shop class 27 years earlier.

Eventually we packed up and left Little Lake to itself. The stream that drains from Little Lake to the Tomorrow River was smoking — I assured the boys that it was healthy smoke. Hardly before I had the car stopped at Jeremy and Jordan's house, Jeremy was out of the car running to the house with the little bucket of panfish and yelling for his mother.

Ten Feet from the Hole — Lance (Age 6), Lukas (Age 5)

Lance opened the chorus with a familiar one: "I got one." Within a minute he was singing again. "Dad, I got another perch." He was hoarse from repeating the "Dad, I got another one," chorus when the noon whistle sent us home for lunch.

Already missing the green towering pine, white birch, rustic oak, white lake, and blue skies, Lance and I returned at dusk. The sun setting in the southwest illuminated the treetops on the northeast shore. The rest of the lake was in a deep shadow. Fingers grew numb; the lines grew stiff, and the tip-ups grew silent while the little perch stole minnow after minnow because lines were frozen in new ice.

Lance abandoned his hole and came over to sit on my lap to share calories that were getting more precious every minute. I caught two bass, which were released, according to our self-imposed rules of Little Lake. Reinspired, Lance got up to try his old hole one more time in the pitch darkness. He lowered the yellow jig and bang — a big fish had it — he jumped up from his bucket and tried hard to see the line in order to guide the fish through the hole. Around and around it went and then when the pole seemed as if it would break, a rainbow popped out and flopped at his feet. He gently reclaimed the teardrop jig and gave the trout back to Little Lake.

Less than a week later, Luke and I returned to Little Lake on another sunny day with each tree on the south side of the lake casting an artistic shadow to the middle of the lake. Luke asked to use Lance's yellow teardrop rather than my purple one. Before I had the first tip-up baited, Luke was yelling at the top of his lungs: "Dad, I got one! I got one!" He dragged the bluegill across the lake for me to unhook and then returned to Lance's 'hot' ice hole.

Suddenly the perch discovered the tip-up. Luke and I ran and ran. Lukas was still learning how to be a Tip-up Man and rarely got to the tip-up soon enough. Finally he learned to watch the flags for early movement and to start running even before the flag was halfway up. Luke ran and ran. I followed with the minnow bucket. Luke pulled and pulled — and sometimes the little perch got the treble hook in the mouth. Luke caught two all by himself.

He was busy counting his fish in his head (2 perch on tip-ups, 2 pumpkinseeds on jigs, and 1 perch on a jig), when the little orange tip-up flag started to wiggle. Lukas jumped from my lap and grabbed the line. He even tried a little hand over hand retrieval. This was a bigger fish that had already run out a lot of line. He decided that the best way to get it out of the water was to walk backwards away from the hole while holding the line as high as possible. The gods reward innocence — an 11 inch perch slid out of the water and squirmed across the ice to see the four foot tall Tip-up Man standing ten feet from the hole.

Lowell Klessig is a professor at the College of Natural Resources, UW-Stevens Point and author of The ELF Odyssey.

Skate On!

MARC EISEN

Some of the most pleasurable moments of my childhood were spent ice-skating in Kenosha County. There was an exhilarating sense of speed, grace and athleticism that sticks with me even today when I strap on a pair of skates as a middle-aged, overweight father of two.

Back then I played hockey on farm ponds far, far away from the world of adults, in that closed universe of kids lost unto themselves. I remember skating breathlessly down the winding Des Plaines River, wondering how far we dared go before turning back in the deepening dusk. I remember big bonfires with flames dancing high into the crisp cold nights, and the first tentative hand-holding with a girl as we skated off into the dark. And I remember the cold.

It was always cold. This was in the days before miracle fibers, before kids wore Sorrel boots, when long underwear was too scratchy to endure. Nothing was more torturous or more agonizing than trudging through a snowy corn field and sitting on a frozen log to lace up skates.

But I loved it despite the hassles. When I finally got my socks unkinked, skates firmly tied and gloves back on, I was in another dimension. Skating was like dreaming. There was that same preternatural sense of flying, of loosening the bonds of gravity, of going whoosh! into the night. I was a kid then and everything was more intense.

For all the usual reasons, I didn't skate again for two decades until I bought a house within a few blocks of Lake Monona in Madison. Did I first head out to the ice because I needed a place to exercise the dog? I don't remember. What I do remember is the freeze of my dreams a year or two later, when Lake Monona turned to ice on an utterly calm night, and the lake shone unblemished as a sheet of Lucite. So much can go wrong when the lake freezes: Wind will leave horrible ridges; snow can ruin everything. But this night the ice was perfection. For miles and miles the ice was clear and unbumped, as if God's own Zamboni had descended from the clouds.

I fell in love with skating again. I remember skating up Starkweather Creek one night that winter with a friend while the ice thinned and cracked (the threat of danger only enhancing the experience), then turning around to race back home under the moonlight. In my mind, we were gliding as surely as Olympians.

Every year I hope in vain for a freeze as good as that. Still, even under mediocre conditions, Lake Monona is a great place to play. When the temperature drops, a 3,274-acre winter wonderland magically springs up in the heart of the city. A refuge on which to hike, ice fish, iceboat, walk the dog, cross-country ski, snowshoe, skate, camp, and gawk at the sky.

To be honest, I'm pretty much a stiff on ice today. Whatever grace I had in my youth has receded with the years. I can wheel around without falling on my face, but my knees strain when I go into a crouch, and the cramps in my feet seem to last longer. Deep down, though, I still believe that my old form will return, if only I could skate daily for a few uninterrupted weeks.

Life conspires against my comeback. With work, family, and my own lassitude, I'm lucky to strap on skates a half-dozen times a year. When I do haul myself out onto the ice, job number one is sticking with my daughters. For many years, the trick was keeping them upright. Now I'm facing the indignity of the eldest outracing me.

Still, I can't complain. One of the pleasures of parenthood is rediscovering the kicks of childhood: skating, sledding, snowmen, sandcastles — the whole endless bag of childish diversions. (Just the other day, as I was sledding with my daughters at Olbrich Park, whooping our way down the hill, snow flying in our faces, I experienced a *frisson* of pleasure that I hadn't felt in years.) The kids turn out to be a great excuse to head for the ice.

If Lake Monona is bad, I'll drag them to Tenney Lagoon on Madison's east side. Like Vilas Lagoon on the west side, Tenney is maintained for skating by the city and has a warming house, concessions and even skate rentals. To go there on a bright, sunny weekend afternoon is to see Madison as Frank Capra might envision it. Everybody is there: Kids flailing around the ice, hovering parents trying to encourage flustered tots, teenage boys jockeying about in packs, solitary men and women cutting figures, rapt lovers, the odd dog.

What's striking is the lack of pretension and the mix of people. So much of sport and recreation today is marked by the emblems of status and exclusion. Even mass spectator sports like baseball and football feature luxury boxes where the rich can separate themselves from ordinary fans. Sports like skiing require expensive equipment and specialized, fashionable clothing.

But skating is different. The barriers aren't there. For a couple of bucks, you can rent a pair of skates for the afternoon. Don't worry if you don't have a fancy Polartec vest. People skate in whatever they wear on the street corner in winter: My sweats are as good as her tights as his jeans as her cords. And everybody drinks the same (bad) hot chocolate sold in the warming house.

It's quite a scene. I love the burble of excitement in the warming house as people sit knee to knee putting on and taking off their skates. It's that "Emersonian crowd feeling," as the late Bart Giamatti, scholar and baseball commissioner, happily put it — people of all ages and backgrounds coming together to enjoy an activity that is both private and public at the same time.

If Tenney Lagoon is democracy at its best, Lake Monona is pure freedom. When the ice is good, you can skate forever — or at least across the lake to the wooded banks of Monona. Once a winter I make that half hour journey, and touch the shoreline for luck. But first I stop smack-dab in the middle and do a slow 360, drinking in the horizon. It's a humbling experience.

The signs of civilization — the Capitol, the huddled houses along the shoreline, the Madison Gas & Electric chimneys — are dwarfed by the great expanse of ice. It's a different world out there, with different signposts. Some stretches appear pitch-black, the murky, bottomless waters looming beneath crystal-clear ice. Other stretches have the look of a Jell-o mold — ice chunks frozen into a crazy fruit salad. And the pressure ridges, with huge frozen slabs jutting into the air and pools of water at the fault line, are sights right out of the tundra.

Every so often you'll hear the slow, rolling thunder of the ice cracking from the pressure (what a grand, ominous sound!). A mile out on the lake, I always pause. For a moment, I'm an 11-year-old boy on a far bend of the Des Plaines River, wondering if the ice will suddenly open up and swallow me. But it doesn't, and I skate on.

Marc Eisen is editor of the Madison weekly, Isthmus.

Grandma's House

S U S A N   L A M P E R T   S M I T H

It's one of those farms on the edge of town, the kind of place that gets surrounded and then swallowed to make way for houses and apartment buildings and Wal-Marts.

This one belongs to my grandparents, so I can visit whenever I like, even though the actual house was bulldozed 20 years ago. That was when the city of Manitowoc decided that a wider street on the developing west edge of town was more important than a cream brick farmhouse.

Sometimes, though, Grandma still thinks she's here. "We have to get upstairs," she told me recently. "We've got a lot of beds to make."

"Don't worry," I said, for once successfully avoiding one of her chores. "I already did it."

My grandma, Elizabeth Zipperer, thinks she's still at the farm because she's had some little strokes, and, more importantly, because once you raise seven girls and a boy on a farm during the Depression, you always think there's more chores to do.

I still think of the old house as being there, too, because I dream it regularly. I'll bet my 25 cousins do, too.

C'mon, I'll give you a virtual tour. The first thing is the smell. It always smells smoky here, because grandma and most of her kids smoke, because of the trash-burning stove in the kitchen, because of the Cher-Make bacon sizzling on the stove. But mostly because of my grandpa, Ed. Ed smokes these cheap cigars that my dad calls "burning overshoes."

Today, when my trendy guy friends light up an expensive stogie after dinner, I want to tell them they smell exactly like a German farmer who snipped his cigars into 2-inch lengths, stuffed them into a corn cob pipe and puffed them as he rammed around on his tractor.

Long after he died the cigars were still with us.

Because it's a farmhouse, the first room is the mud room. This is where the little kids eat at Thanksgiving, where the dads play poker, and where Grandpa keeps cases of orange soda that came in little brown bottles.

Next is the kitchen. Everything happens here. Some of girls were born here on the kitchen table. Now they are moms themselves, each more dark-haired, beautiful and disputatious than the next. (Imagine, seven girls in one family!) It is always very loud here, especially on Sundays after church when polka music booms from the radio and everyone crowds into the kitchen to visit.

At dinner, you always try to sit next to Grandpa, because he shows off for the kids. You never know if he'll take out his false teeth or mix his salad into his spaghetti because "it all goes to the same place anyway."

You do know Grandpa doesn't think much of Vatican II watering down the prayers to talk about some little pansy called the Holy Spirit. Grace said by Grandpa ends like this: "In the name of the vater, the son und the HOLY GHOST. (Slam! The fist hits the table! The dishes jump!) Let's eat."

Next is the living room. Nothing interesting happens here, because the uncles are always telling you to get out of the way of the Packer game.

Now, the stairs are interesting. There's 80 zillion pictures of the family here. You always check to see if your mother in her bright red lipstick graduation picture is as pretty as her six sisters in theirs and if there's as many pictures of you as of your cousins. If there isn't, you tell your mom. She'll do something about it.

The other important thing about the stairs is that they turn, so you can sit here late at night when you are supposed to be in bed and listen to the card-playing, the hollering, and the arguing coming from the kitchen.

At the top of the stairs is the bedroom where you never want to sleep — and not just because you once threw up here after eating an entire bag of orange marshmallow circus peanut candies. It's got the door to the attic, where the bad thing lives.

Worse, from the window you can see the fog from Lake Michigan swirling under the yardlight.

Grandma says the horrible moaning noise is just the foghorn, but you know it's the thing in the attic, coming to get you.

The animals are mostly gone by the mid-1960s, but the granary is still fun. Cousin Sherry and I like to drag out piles of dress-up clothes (seven sisters leave a legacy of lace and satin behind) and play queens in our dusty realm, locking our brothers outside. I think this is where she convinced me to drink a bottle of holy water, telling me I would never have another sore throat. It tastes like liquid dust, in case you wonder.

When you're a kid, it's easier to know your grandma's house than your grandma.

The older I get, the more I wonder what it was like to run a farm while your husband, worked at the dairy plant in town, to have a new baby nearly every year during the 1930s.

The 1930s! When even the rich were poor and when those horrible broiling summers of the Dust Bowl returned every year. Each July, I cringe when I read that Wisconsin's never-equaled high temperature of 107 degrees came in July 1935, the month my mother, the middle sister, was born.

"How did you do it?" I've asked Grandma, more than once, trying to picture myself in her shoes.

"We all did it," she'll say. "Everyone did."

Sometime Grandma's house gives up clues about her life. In the attic, we discover the love letters grandpa wrote to her. She was done with school in eighth grade, and sent down to Milwaukee to work as a cook and maid in the fine homes along the lake.

That's where she learned so many of her famous recipes. And my grandpa would wait for her train when she came home for visits. His letters were signed "Love, Eddie."

We recently celebrated Grandma's 90th birthday at her new house, the St. Mary's Home for the Aged. Because we're now a huge group, with the great-grandkids and all, we took over the auditorium. There was polka music and my aunts made the foods we always had at Grandma's, the homemade dill pickles and the peanut squares.

Grandpa is long dead, there's an apartment building in his pea field and a pre-fab home where the old brick farmhouse once stood. But one thing hasn't changed from those gatherings back in the farmhouse kitchen: we're still a loud and boisterous group. I hope the other nursing home residents didn't mind. Maybe they sat on the stairs and listened.

Susan Lampert Smith writes "On Wisconsin" *for the* Wisconsin State Journal, *where a version of this story appeared. She is the author of* Greetings from Wisconsin.

Time, Rock, Water

PAUL G. HAYES

It appears illogical an a map. Two streams approach each other, the main stem of the Milwaukee River from the north, its tributary, Cedar Creek, from the west. It looks as though they will merge momentarily, but with less than two miles to close, Cedar Creek, now trending northeast, abruptly turns south more than 90 degrees. Now the two streams run parallel for about three miles. Coursing through the settlement of Cedarburg, Cedar Creek again turns east and again promises to join the river after it falls over the five dams of Cedarburg, its hydraulic power having grown, but its strength still dictated by seasonal fluctuations of precipitation and spring thaw. The creek approaches to within two hundred yards of the river but it turns away again. On the map, the two streams, before they merge at last a mile east of Cedarburg, flow through a broad flood plain. So smoothed, their waters silently slip into a single stream.

One must walk the land and canoe both streams to understand this waffling of watery will. The answer lies in the limestone bedrock, as deep as 150 feet in many places, but which protrudes through the surface occasionally.

The Milwaukee River rises a good distance west of Fond du Lac County and moves east, but limestone turns it south so that it runs parallel to the lake shore, as close to it as a mile. The river breaks through to the lake at Milwaukee harbor. This same limestone rises east of Cedarburg forming the dense wall that turns aside Cedar Creek a couple of times before it merges with the river.

The limestone bears fossil life that teemed in shallow salt seas that covered much of what is now the state of Michigan more than 400 million years ago. Its western edge forms the peninsula that is Wisconsin's Door County and the ridges that extend southward through all of eastern Wisconsin and into Illinois. In eastern Wisconsin the layered rock has been lifted so that it tilts eastward, forming the west rim of a stone saucer, a subterranean dish that has become filled in with all of the later rocks and all of the soil and all of the life that is now the state of Michigan. The east rim of the dish surfaces again at Buffalo, New York where it is the ledge over which the Niagara River falls.

Some of that water spent a century circulating in the cul-de-sac that is

Lake Michigan and some of it once flowed in Cedar Creek behind my house, but so many decades ago that I never directly looked upon it nor experienced it in any way. When it was in the creek, the five Cedarburg dams were young, even though we think of them now as pioneer artifacts dating from the first years of the statehood. In eastern Wisconsin the Niagara dolomite directed a slow ballet that shaped everything we see. It dictated the shape of Lake Michigan and it helped set the route of the Milwaukee River. The dense wedge of dolomite that now is Door County split the glacier as the ice sheet advanced southward, with one lobe of ice shoveling out Lake Michigan, the other gouging out Green Bay, Lake Winnebago and the depression that filled up to become Horicon Marsh. The Milwaukee River formed along the west edge of the Lake Michigan lobe as the ice melted.

When the Milwaukee ran in front of the glacier it briefly may have been a mighty river and it helped fill glacial Lake Chicago, which now has receded to become the southern basin of Lake Michigan. What I see in my imagination is a craggy range of ice, lying in the lake, deep gullies cut into its west flank by melt water, the ice glowing a morning-glory blue in the sun, torrents washing down the gullies to form the river. I see black spruce groves taking root as the glacier recedes, and these attract mammoth, mastodon and caribou, and these in turn attract bands of human hunters from the south. When I spade my garden in spring, I find chips of white chert; my neighbor has picked arrowheads from his. When I replace posts for my grape arbor, my post-hole digger penetrates a of layer of golden sand starting at a foot and a half down. I have never dug to the bottom of it. I envision an ice age beach on Cedar Creek, a nice encampment for an artisan sitting in the sun chipping at a flint.

I sit on a bench at the end of a short pier that extends my back yard into a shallow, silt-bottomed pond between two of Cedarburg's dams. If it is a hot August day, I watch the torpedo-shaped shadows of carp. If it is September, I watch cedar waxwings burst from the willow snag high above me, grab a flying insect and return to its branch. I watch the flock explode a second before the sharp-shinned hawk alights in the snag.

If it is an October dusk, I watch the nightly reunion at the pond of the families of giant Canada geese as they return from Ozaukee County cornfields. For as long as the pond remains unfrozen, these geese spend the night gossiping raucously behind my house. If the pond freezes, they'll move temporarily to Lake Michigan to sit on open water. But they won't migrate.

Sixty or so strokes of the canoe paddle west, I come to the rapids where Cedar Greek falls over three or four steps of bedded limestone, experiencing just a hint of what's in store for it at Niagara Falls 700 miles east and more than a century downstream. Beyond the rapids I see the water-draped face of Ruck dam, the water falling from the millpond 10 feet above. The Hilgen-Schroeder grist mill looms to my left, constructed in 1855 of blocks that were quarried from the creek bed in front of my canoe.

Upstream from Ruck dam is the Woolen Mill dam, a 12-foot fall from the creek as it runs past Boy Scout park. In cold Winters, the pond above is the town's skating rink. In hot summers, it yields bullheads. Downstream from Ruck dam are three more dams, an 11-foot fall over Columbia Mill dam, a 26-foot fall over Nail Factory dam, a 7-foot fall over Hamilton dam. Four stone mills still stand near the dams; only Columbia Mill, which was a huge red frame building, decayed to the point of no return in the 1960s. None of the buildings is a working mill; they are shops, offices, warehouses; all of them are treasured artifacts.

In Madison, at the Department of Natural Resources, there is a conviction that old dams in Wisconsin pose varying degrees of hazard and that their removal will improve the quality of water and fishing along the streams. But where else in Wisconsin, indeed where in the world, are there five pioneer dams in only two and a half miles? Improve the fishing perhaps, but lose the history, the essence of this place, and banish forever the happy ghosts that haunt Cedarburg. Where the limestone delles confine the creek, above Nail Factory dam and Columbia Mill dam, white cedar trees flourish, and their roots fill limestone crevasses, clutching the rock like talons explaining the name of my town, where I sit on a bench a few inches above the water, watch carp, hear geese and think on these things.

Paul G. Hayes retired as an award-winning environmental reporter for the Milwaukee Journal *in 1995, sharing in a Pulitzer Prize for a series on water pollution.*

Louis No.1

TOM HOLLATZ

Louis St. Germaine of Lac du Flambeau, Wisconsin, who was known as "Louis No. 1" for his guiding prowess, was born in 1898. He was abandoned by his parents as a nine-year-old lad with his younger brother on the shores of White Sand Lake with only a sack of flour to sustain them.

It was fall.

A November wind was a razor cutting to the bone of the inhabitants of the Wisconsin Northwoods. The trees were now barren of leaves except for the stingy oak brown leaves which always drop to the earth in spring. Blue-gray clouds muscled their way across the Lac du Flambeau Indian reservation as young Louis and his brother watched in tears as their parents walked away. History of the event has faded as to the whys of the abandonment. Trees, too, never apologize for shedding leaves.

It was on that sandy anvil that Louis St. Germaine forged one of the great guiding careers in outdoor history. Louis had been told that he would find life in Mother Earth which provided strawberries, raspberries, blackberries, marsh cranberries and the good things like wild rice.

He also discovered that the many lakes in the Northwoods contain a bounty of fish for him to catch. And he became quite good at it. Soon lumberjacks hired young Louis to take them fishing and tourists, too, realized that Louis was something special and started calling him "Louis No. 1" because there were several guides with the same name.

Louis was also a great athlete. He was sent to Carlisle College where he played with the great Jim Thorpe. Homesick for the Northwoods, he returned to his home where his legend continued to grow. It was rumored he was Olympic material, but refused to leave his beautiful Northwoods.

Louis had simpler ambitions.

And then he had a chance to meet another sports legend, the baseball great Ted Williams. A lover of fishing and the outdoors, Williams just had to visit the North and meet this Ojibwa guide known as "Louis No. 1." It was friendship at first cast. Their friendship became lifelong.

When I was going to write the book about "Louis No. 1" I knew I had to contact Ted Williams. I heard he was a "difficult" person. I tried. And then a letter arrived from Islamorada, Florida. It was from Ted. It was a kind and generous letter about Louis St. Germaine.

My favorite picture is of Louie and Ted sharing a joke while relaxing at a shore lunch. Here were the best of their individual worlds sharing a day of fishing and friendship.

They tell the story of when Williams was the outdoors representative for Sears working in the sports department of a Minneapolis Sears store. He was surrounded by a crowd of well-wishers and the Sears' suits. Suddenly, Ted turned his gaze to someone entering the store with his wife and small children. It was Louis St. Germaine. Ted pushed the suits and glad handers aside and ran to Louis and his small family where he hugged them all.

Louis' legend continued to grow. Anglers would follow him, some used spyglasses from the shore to learn his techniques. To foil the spies, he'd wear a red shirt out and as he rounded the bend on White Sand Lake, he'd reverse it and now had on a green shirt.

Louis died at the age of 84. When he passed away at the Howard Young Medical Center in Woodruff, he donated his eyes.

Nope, the walleyes aren't safe.

Tom Hollatz is the author of numerous books on fishing, camp cooking, and Northwood legends. He writes from Boulder Junction.

The Milwaukee
Three Rivers Watershed

RICK WHALEY

The waters of life have always been here. The Devonian Sea covered Milwaukee and the upper Midwest. The corals and shells of gastropods that lived there broke down and over the eons became the fossilized dolomitic limestone that would eventually bring the settlers of the European line here along with industrial capital.

The limestone caves here were attractive to the German beer barons who, in the days before refrigeration, used them to cold-store the liquid that would make Milwaukee famous. More importantly, limestone is that magic stone powder that in blast furnaces is the flux that catalyzes metals to fuse — giving us the great manufacturing era of foundries, mills and factories that once made Milwaukee "the machine shop of the world." Limestone is also the binding material in concrete and mortar used to erect this era's dwellings - schools, monuments and the famous Cream City brick homes.

The factories and foundries of Milwaukee's industrial era, indebted to those Devonian minerals, provided jobs to wave after wave of those fleeing the 19th century religious persecutions in mainland Europe, the flares of Ireland, and the political conquests there.

It was the glaciers, two million to 10,000 years ago, and what grew here when the great sheets of ice melted away, that brought the first indigenous peoples here. Nine thousand years ago, the first hunters followed the mastodons north as the glaciers retreated. Mound builders were here creating over 200 ceremonial mounds in the shape of panthers, lizards, foxes, and spirit animals.

Our bioregion's three rivers - the Milwaukee, the Menomonee, the Kinnickinic — have always been a gathering place of nations. The Menominees were here 5000 years ago, followed by the Mesquaki, Potawatomi, Huron, Ottowa, Miamis, Ho Chunk and Chippewa. By the time Solomon Juneau arrived, native peoples raced horses on the beaches of Lake Michigan, gathered wild rice in the swamp that is now downtown Milwaukee, and harvested the salmon and trout that swam up the three rivers in the tens of thousands. The Menominee named themselves for the wild rice that grew from the harbor up the Menomonee River cedar-tamarack swamp. The Kinnickinic was named for the Native ceremonial tobacco (toasted willow or sumac bark). The name Milwaukee could have come from many sources, but the most inspiring was the Potawatomi, "gathering place by the waters." These three rivers that make up our bioregion's basin, our watershed, flow into the "Michigami" - our great body of water — Lake Michigan.

The air and water and land still make community with the people, but in hard ways - the cycle of abuse returned. Lead in the soil poisons children's blood and learning abilities. You can't eat the PCB fish in Lake Michigan, our drinking water source. The air is so bad on ozone-alert summer days that old people and others with compromised immune systems die, like in the cryptosporidium water crisis of 1993. Asthma attacks are the greatest single reason children are admitted to emergency hospital care in our urban-sprawled metropolis.

Other imbalances of greed — the manufacturing layoffs, disinvestments overseas, and robotization of the early 1980s — killed the heydays of Milwaukee skilled jobs. Gangs, crack cocaine and home foreclosures followed, then the white-collar layoffs of the 1990s. In the most segregated city in the country, 50 percent of the young Black men in our urban core are unemployed. People are the greatest resource being wasted in the City.

With this sense of urgency, we celebrate the sacredness of all our communities, human and natural, and call for their defense. We also rally for a vision of our place beyond everybody-gets-a-piece-of-the-pie politics. Already, Hmong gardens dot the city. AmeriCorps Service Corps sells organic produce at inner city markets. Purple cone flowers return to wild edges and to planned prairie yards. People re-consecrate old trees and green spaces in an effort to preserve nature places in the city — for the renewal of human spirits and as survival corridors for other species. Milwaukee's factories and skilled labor base could build light rail cars, the infrastructure for renewable energy industries and for modest-scale agricultural equipment and processing again.

This is where you live, in the Milwaukee three river's bioregion on the shore of a damaged Great Lake, in a city of neighborhoods struggling to save itself and find the beauty that was always here.

Rick Whaley is a Green activist in Milwaukee, and author of Walleye Warriors. *His essay is adapted from a presentation made to AmeriCorps training.*

Mother Earth

MIKE MOSSMAN

I don't know how many lives I had passed through before this, but here I was in Baxter's Hollow once again. I've had many journeys here, in this place which I can no longer distinguish from myself — the place that is both comfort and mystery, challenge and rest, old and new, inside me and encompassing me, dream and awake, timeless and immediate. Here I have died of old age and of my own despair, I have been reborn, and I have discovered things that I did not understand until years or lifetimes later.

Now I was high up in a red oak tree on the forested end of a small, quartzite ridge. This was the ridge from which I watched turkey-vultures those many early mornings from a blind made of stout limbs and old fenceposts, which the 20 intervening years have laid gently down to meld with the forest soil, like my bones. This is also where I once saw an immortal old man puttering about his home within the rocky ground. It is early in fall now, and I find that I am a leaf made by the old magic of this tree, from the earth's rich elements, its water, and from the air that moves through the forest and over my green body.

As the days progress, the insects that held to my underside with tiny barbed feet eventually disappear to the forest floor far below, into the crevices of bark and rock. Slowly, I become aware that my sap and leaf-alchemy are being drawn back into the tree that had originally given them to me and thus made me alive. I become gradually brittle and for a while tinged with red and yellow-orange. Then, as I fade to brown the tree loosens its grasp, letting go of me not out of disregard, but from an ancient impulse, which is part of a wisdom much beyond the tree or me, and which guides our journeys. Now is my one inevitable release and fall. In falling, I know that it gives life, just as my own life was made possible by the falling of my ancestors I am joining an old traditional dance, which is familiar and fills me, while at the same time I am releasing all that I own, all security, all control.

During this dance to the earth, my senses, thoughts, and feelings are very lucid, and it occurs to me that I have just been born — the umbilicus severed — at the same time that I am dying; that I am passing through the world and deeper into it.

I land on the earth, which is already covered by the thin golden leaves of sugar maples, and the breeze tumbles me over them until at last I rest where the wind leaves me. A strange feeling it is for a leaf to find itself resting on its back, waiting with its stem in the air. I wait here until another wind bounds over the forest floor, around the trees and rocks, and tumbles me again.

Then, there is cold rain and soon I find myself suspended in a swollen stream, moving fitfully as the water rushes me between purple rocks, gray detached limbs, green moss, and yellow mats of maple leaves. The water becomes crystal-clear and I sink to the bottom of a small, cool, luminous pool. I stay here for 3 days, the sky above me changing between gray, blue, and starry black.

On the fourth day the earth moves slightly beneath me, and my invisible, watery medium ever so slightly lifts and jostles me. Above the pool, at its edge, a person appears. She squats beside the pool and after a moment her gaze comes to rest on me. She reaches into the pool, the water on her hand and arm feeling as it would on her throat if she were thirsty. I am grasped between her fingers and pulled up and out of the water, back into the air and closer to her clear, unpresuming gaze. She has dark hair and smooth skin with the faint lines of smiles at the corners of her eyes.

I remain with her during the ensuing days as she walks along the stream and among the purple boulders and ledges of the forest, gathering mosses, dry leaves, mushrooms, roots and nuts. She brings these things back to the stream, where the roots of a yellow birch tree wind in and out of the rocky, mossy bank. Among these roots is an opening like that of a winter wren's nest, lined with mosses. She takes these things into it, into a small, low, but comfortable cavity with a ceiling of intertwining birch roots and a floor of rocks over which she has laid layers of leaves and moss.

The leaves on the forest floor are now dry. The sky turns gray for several days and releases a fine mist, which makes the forest very close and peaceful, manifesting many details of color, texture, and smell. The leaves soften again, and some begin to decay. Yet I remain strong and supple, even increasingly so. Now I am glad that she took me from the pool, and I have developed some devotion to her, and feel honored to help clothe her.

There are then several days of clear weather, during which the woman travels and collects quite extensively. Then the sky darkens again. She now sits on a rock outcrop where she has often slept — for since I have been with her she has entered her den only to bring in and arrange the materials she has collected. The outcrop overlooks the den, from a distance.

In the first light of day she is sitting, carefully watching as the snow begins to accent the purple rocks and the surface textures of tree trunks and branches, and to dust her hair with starry flakes. Before it begins to accumulate on the ground, she descends to the stream, walks along it to the birch tree, and quickly stoops and enters her den.

Mike Mossman lives in Sauk County and writes extensively on Wisconsin's birds. He is co-author of Breeding Birds of the Baraboo Hills.

Badger

RON LEYS

The question before the house today is whether it is politically correct to make sport of one of our wild citizens in order to sell tickets to football games.

The wild citizen is our beloved badger, and the sportmaker I speak of is none other than that guy in a funny costume who calls himself Bucky Badger. You know the guy I mean — the one who puffs out his chest and pulls his face into a fierce scowl and struts back and forth at Camp Randall Stadium and across our television screens. Is this fair?

The question haunted me for days after a happening on a warm afternoon when I had been trudging up a steep, grassy hill for too long — my attention had been on the ground in front of me, my mind on how hot and tired I was, when a sudden loud hiss made me forget all that.

I looked up, and not ten feet to my right were three wild critters. Big guys, with distinctive striped faces and gray bodies, bigger than one expects to see in wild animals. They could only be badgers. The biggest of them was hissing at me in a decidedly unfriendly fashion. Then they scuttled away, looking like big shovel blades with scurrying feet.

I was, to put it mildly, dumbfounded.

For upward of 50 years, I had been roaming the woods and fields of Wisconsin, but the only places I had ever seen badgers were on flags, on posters and in that funny suit at football games back in my University of Wisconsin undergrad days. I had seen just about every kind of wild mammal found in the state, along with most birds, but I had never seen a wild badger in the Badger State.

There had once been a bunch of them in a cage in the Vollrath Park Zoo, a block from my boyhood home in Sheboygan. And I remember watching in fascination as those badgers hissed at each other and scuttled back and forth. Next to Sadie the lion, they were about my favorite animals.

But in my old age, I was beginning to doubt that wild badgers were still around Wisconsin, if they ever had been.

Sure, we live in the Badger State and one of those fellows is on our state flag above the sailor and the miner. But I knew that was because lead miners of the early 1800s had become known as badgers because of the holes they dug, and sometimes lived in, in the hillsides of south central Wisconsin. Or perhaps, as suggested by Reginald Horsman of the UW-Milwaukee in a letter to the Wisconsin Magazine of History, the miners became known as badgers because they were seen as rough and rowdy characters.

Almost all those miners had come from somewhere else, and it had occurred to me that their knowledge of badgers and the holes they dig might have been picked up elsewhere and simply applied to the Wisconsin scene they found themselves in — the Wisconsin badger might well be as mythical as the unicorn.

But now the proof otherwise had been in front of my eyes. Badgers do live free in the Badger State.

Indeed, my copy of Hartley H. T. Jackson's Mammals of Wisconsin says badgers are found throughout Wisconsin, but nowhere are they plentiful. Although I had seen three together, badgers are normally solitary animals, not even liking other badgers very much most times, and Jackson says two or three to a square mile would be considered a high badger population.

They are mainly active at night, and are usually known to be about by the piles of dirt they throw up as they vigorously dig after mice and gophers and such.

So now that we know that the badger is a real creature with a real life, how does that change how we feel about the phony animal that infests football stadiums, sweatshirts and beer glasses and the like?

Should we apologize to the real badger for taking its likeness in vain? For making sport of a life that it seems to take pretty seriously?

If we can't have fanciful Indian braves with tomahawks representing our athletic teams any more, why can we make a cartoon character of this just-as-real creature?

It took a while, and some sleepless nights, let me tell you, to come to a solution, but it finally came to me.

I think there are three basic reasons why it's OK to mimic the badger. One: It is a fierce individual that one antagonizes at one's peril, just like a University of Wisconsin football team in some years; a prudent person would no more poke a stick in a badger's face than he would in a middle linebacker's face. Two: The badger doesn't know that we are using its image. Three: If it did know, it wouldn't give a damn.

Perhaps even more than most other animals, the badger lives its own life. It eats animals smaller than itself, and pays no attention to those bigger. Quaking in fear and worrying about things is something that rabbits and mice and possums do, not badgers.

So go ahead, laugh at the antics of Bucky Badger at the next UW football game, and go ahead, strut like Bucky if our guys in red and white should happen to win.

The real Bucky couldn't care less.

Ron Leys retired from the Milwaukee Journal *and now lives and writes in Gays Mills. He is co-author of* Favorite Fishing Spots of Southeast Wisconsin.

Hidden Madison

BILL LUEDERS

All my life I've looked for them, these hidden places. Places that hardly anybody knows about. Places where you can go to be the only person to be found. Places where nature is being left more or less alone.

When I was a teenager in Milwaukee, my favorite such place was called Havenwoods — a square mile of land in the heart of the city's north side. Old sidewalks and parking lots (from the days when this area housed military barracks) slowly crumbled back to earth as grasses and saplings took root in the slightest of cracks. Long-forgotten trails wound over hills and through wooded areas.

Alas, Havenwoods is hidden no more — A few years back the state Department of Natural Resources transformed it into a state forest, complete with a museum and concessions stand. Now groups of schoolchildren walk nature trails along paths my dog and I once had to ourselves.

Since moving to Madison in 1986, I've checked out much of the city in search of other hidden spots, and I've discovered quite a few. These are tracts of land that the city — if not time — seems to have forgotten. Most are visited by neighborhood residents, and some are special enough to attract people from other parts of town. But none are well-known. That's part of their charm.

And so it is with some trepidation that I present this list of a dozen of my favorite hidden places in Madison. I know, it doesn't make sense: What possible motive could I have for revealing places whose main attraction is that so few people are aware of them?

The truth is that I just can't help myself. As a journalist, it's my job to find things that are hidden and bring them to light. It's pathetic.

Besides, if you're the kind of person who loves to check out the nooks and crannies of the city in which you live, then I guess you're guilty of no greater offense than I. Happy hidden trails to you.

The Grady Tract: Relatively few Arboretum visitors come to this spectacular 195-acre parcel of woodland and prairie situated south of the Beltline. (This includes the world-renowned Greene Prairie, now at risk due to planned development just outside the park.)

The tract is surrounded almost entirely with a six-foot-high chain-link fence and accessible, notes Arboretum director Greg Armstrong, "only to those people who are willing to spend energy to walk into it." There are just two points of entry. One is a small parking lot on Seminole Highway just south of the Beltline. Or you can park in the lot across from Curtis Prairie, take a path through the prairie, and to the right that will take you to — I swear I'm not making this up — a tunnel that runs underneath the Beltline to the other side.

Knollwood Conservation Park: Adjacent to the Grady Tract but not accessible from it is a linear stretch of thick woods nestled between a railroad track on one side and Arbor Hills residences on the other. One gorgeous summer evening, I trudged through here for more than an hour and never saw another soul. In fact, the paths were so overgrown I wondered if I was the first person since, like, Nicolet, to actually set foot here.

Take the frontage road south of the Beltline between Seminole Highway and Todd Drive, turn on Grandview Boulevard, go right on Sandwood Way and left on Westview Lane. The park entrance is a block up the street; if you blink, you'll miss it. Almost immediately, you'll have to cross a thin stream by balancing on narrow logs. Then head left to a wooden boardwalk and trails beyond.

Governor's Island: It seems somehow appropriate that this natural jewel named after the state's highest constitutional office isn't really an island at all but a peninsula (come to think of it, I've never seen the governor here either). Trails along lakeshore bluffs offer views of Lake Mendota and opportunities to fall to one's death. Other trails cut through the heart of the island.

Take Cinder Drive from the grounds of Mendota Mental Health Institute, itself a premium piece of real estate. (Bonus place: My favorite point of entry to this larger area is a tiny trail along the lake that begins where Woodward Drive meets Harper Road.)

Owen Conservation Park: A friend of mine who has this 100-acre nature preserve practically in his backyard is going to be none too pleased I'm letting others in on his little secret. But this west-side wonder is simply one of the most lovely, secluded places to be found in the midst of this or any other city.

The park is accessible by foot from several areas, including Inner Drive, and by car off Old Sauk Road across the street from Crestwood School. The road leads to a parking lot, where newcomers can view maps and aerial photos before hitting the trails. If you meet a guy named Dave, don't tell him I sent you.

Starkweather Creek Path: This is a mile-long bike/hike path that runs from the Shopko store off Aberg Avenue all the way to MATC. Intersecting dirt trails lead to sizable patches of undeveloped land and various points of neighborhood access. Most of this land — including the MATC baseball park — is owned by the county as airport right-of-way.

The new path connects a loose network of existing paths. One spur picks up at East Johnson by Fourth Street and runs through Demetral Park to North Street; then Kedzie Street will take you to Shopko and the new bike path. The path ends at Anderson Street, which runs to Highway 51, where another path starts on Lien Road behind the PDQ, runs through Reindahl Park and lets out on Portage Road right by East Towne.

Frautschi Point: Just about everybody and their cousin have been to Picnic Point off University Bay Drive, but few venture forth on the property that winds north and west along the lake. This includes a 17-acre chunk of formerly private and still-pristine land donated to the university by the Frautschi family in 1989.

Stay on the path closest to the lake, and soon you'll find yourself in thick woods overlooking lakeshore bluffs, with trails that cut back into the heart of the property. After about a mile, you'll come to a small parking lot just down the street from the entrance to Eagle Heights.

Heistand Park: This 46.5 acre patch of city parkland off Milwaukee Street just past Highway 51 was originally a federal radar site for Truax Field and the planned site for a never-built hospital. Go past the old school and tennis court, past the huge boulders strewn on the narrow path and up a long winding hill to one of the best vistas in town.

In 1998, the city Parks Division built a Frisbee golf course at Heistand, but trails still lead to plenty of secluded areas.

Turville Woods: Every day, thousands of Madisonians pass this urban gem along John Nolen Drive, and my guess is that only a handful have any idea what is back here. What's back here is 65 acres of city parkland, including an eight-acre prairie. A series of interconnecting trails wind through wooded areas and along the lake.

Turville Woods has been tarred by media accounts of gay men using the area for anonymous encounters. The faint of heart may want to stick to the area along the lake and adjacent to Olin Park, although I've been all over this park many times and the only sex I've seen is between birds. I'm not sure if it was anonymous.

Edna Taylor Conservation Park: The next time you're out saving big money at the Monona Menards, stop off at this pretty preserve just off Femrite Drive. "It's one of my favorite places," attests Russ Hefty, city conservation manager for the Madison Parks Division, which owns just over half the 100-acre parcel. (The rest is in Monona and is said to be that city's last remaining chunk of undeveloped land.)

Trails lead through prairies, savannas and wetlands up into a wooded hillside. The park also boasts a number of Indian effigy mounds, only a few of which were destroyed by developers of a planned new subdivision.

Prairie Ridge Conservation Park: This is the city's newest park, on the burgeoning southwest side. It's address is 2406 Berkeley, a street so new it's not even on my map. The easiest way to get there is to take Whitney Way to Raymond Road, turn left on Muir Field Road and pull over by the sign that says Raymond Ridge Park. The conservation park starts at the top of the hill.

Stand on the top of the hill, and look west, and all you can see is farmland for miles and miles. Look east, and you'll see rolling hills of houses that also seem to stretch on forever. This place stands defiant against a sea of sprawl. May it hold its ground.

Sycamore Park: One of just four city parks that allow dogs to be off-leash, this former landfill on Madison's east side is a pleasant, wide-open space. (Torn up in 1998, the park should reopen in early 1999.) It's a great place to toss a Frisbee or fly a kite, with a nice mile-long trail and a few steep hills to climb, yet it's almost always deserted, save for the people who come to shovel free wood chips from a pile in the parking lot. It's worth checking out, especially in the evening as the sun goes down. Take East Washington Ave. to Mendota Street by K-mart to Sycamore.

Lakeview Woods: Wanna get high? One of the city's highest points and best views — on a clear day when the leaves are off the trees you can see four Madison lakes — can be had from the Dane County Human Services building, 1202 Northport Dr. But you can get even higher by going past the garage and maintenance building to a trailhead that begins by the old water tower — from here, paths crisscross a densely wooded 27-acre county conservation park.

Years ago when the building was a sanitarium, says county park director Ken LePine, these woods were "part of the therapy." They're still a sanity enhancer today. Stay to the left and you'll come out in a clearing by a little cemetery so pretty the living may indeed envy the dead-

There's also a lovely chapel, "Saint John's Evangelical Lutheran Church," built in 1884.

Bill Lueders is news editor of Isthmus, *where a version of this article originally appeared, and author of* An Enemy of the State: The Life of Erwin Knoll.

The Forgotten Land

MICHAEL VAN STAPPEN

One early spring morning I drove far down the slushy back roads to an old riveted steel bridge that had been built sometime between the two world wars. Along the way, I could see that winter's blanket of snow was quickly melting away. The weather had recently been unseasonably seasonable, which is to say that early spring weather in Lake Superior country has all the predictability of an earthquake, and sometimes a similar, though milder, effect on our lives.

The engineer who designed the bridge placed it a short distance downstream from the confluence of Pine and North Fish Creeks. At the bridge, I leaned over a rusty riveted rail and watched a boiling brown slurry of water, ice, mud, branches, and twigs, rushing madly beneath the bridge. Above the water's roar, every so often I heard strange, dull thuds. These were most likely the sounds of large stones or small boulders smacking other rocks as they grudgingly tumbled along the bottom, levered downstream by the sheer force of high spring flow.

Peering downstream, I began to see how North Fish Creek had etched itself into this steep-sided valley of its own making. Melting snow and rainwater from fields and forests hundreds of feet above funnel down into countless small ravines. These in turn lead to larger ravines which finally empty into the creek. Once the snow starts melting and spring rains begin to fall, it doesn't take long for all this water to find the creek. In a matter of days, this humble stream crescendos to a torrent, carving its way ever deeper into the landscape.

If glacial geologists are right, it seems the life of North Fish Creek must have started about 8500 years ago. At this time, a great lobe of the Wisconsin glacial sheet, which had covered this area for thousands of years, began to melt and recede. Geologists called it the Chippewa Lobe. As this immense, decaying ice sheet withdrew, several lakes formed in its wake. As the ice continued retreating northward into what is now Canada, the surface level of this Lake Duluth began falling in stages. Eventually it reached a level close to that of modern day Lake Superior.

Here along the North Coast a new landscape born of ice and water had emerged. Most of the lowlands, formerly glacial lake bottoms, were covered deeply with iron-rich clay that came from the melting glacier. Ancient sand beaches formed in places along the shorelines of these glacial lakes.

Above the reach of the glacial lakes, the broad highland that runs the length of the Bayfield Peninsula was more directly shaped by the receding ice front. Here the dry, sandy land reads like a textbook of glacial features: kettles and potholes, recessional moraines, pitted outwash plains, braided streambeds. It is a land apart from the rest, with dry forests and openings that are prone to fire, and a topography that defies common sense to all but geologists. These unique features are the very underpinning of the unique ecosystems we call the barrens. It is difficult enough to comprehend — much less believe it possible that such a parched landscape was born of ice and water.

Most of us living here today are oblivious to the epic drama out of which Lake Superior and the North Coast country was reborn. It was a rebirth not by fire but by ice — a horrendous rending and reshaping of a new landscape by the vast and distant energies of the atmosphere and oceans. Evidence of this great rebirth is everywhere underfoot. It is the very underpinning of our existence here today. To see it, we need only to look.

I waded upstream to a place where I could cross without risk of quicksand or over-topping my waders. Moving downstream again along the bank, I saw that the reddish layers were not clay but sand. The red color was from mineral iron in the sand that had oxidized; the clay here is red for the same reason. But how did the sand get way out here and way down beneath all that glacial clay? Looking again at the layers, I thought of how the glacial clay and till rest atop the sandstone all along the coast and throughout the Apostle Islands. Rubbing the sugary sand between my fingers, I realized that the layers were weathered sandstone, not sediments from the glaciers but from another, immensely distant place and time.

Digging with my fingers in the soil just above the sandstone layers, I found clay, and it was indeed resting upon the sandstone. There is no physical distance between the clay and sandstone, yet in time the distance is more than a billion years. Standing there in waders, with a big fly rod in my hand and the purling water flowing around me, I felt strangely displaced. It was as if I could feel the sweep of time and events swirling endlessly onward around me. I wondered if this was what it was like to be a rock, or to die and be still, to watch the world forever fading into the future. This rock obviously has a good head start on the rest of us.

A few days later I was thinking again about the sandstone and the vast gap in time represented by the overlying glacial sediments. In that billion years, life as we know it had arisen from some prototype single cell organism and evolved to the great diversity of life on earth today. Other sediments, or at times lava and other volcanic material, had been deposited on top of this sandstone, only to be eroded away. At some time dinosaurs must have roamed the ceaselessly changing landscapes that had existed here. But there are no fossil dinosaur bones to be found because they were also eroded away. All that remains today of these lost landscapes are questions that may never be completely answered. Those questions are sandwiched right there between the sandstone and glacial clay. We could come here any time we like and lay our hands on them and wonder.

Michael Van Stappen lives near the Wisconsin shores of Lake Superior. This essay is taken from his recent book, Northern Passages.

In the Footsteps of John Muir

MILLIE STANLEY

I live in the land of John Muir's boyhood and youth. My land lies on the southern edge of Marquette County a few miles from John Muir Memorial Park where the Muirs settled in 1849 and one half mile from the Muirs' second farm, Hickory Hill. When I climb the ridge I can see the Hickory Hill farmhouse in the distance. Down my road is the farm where the family first stayed when they scouted for land. The site of the school house John attended briefly one winter is just over the hill.

When the Muir family came from Scotland and settled in Marquette County they immediately put up a shanty for shelter, cleared land for crops, and built their home. They named Fountain Lake and their farm after it.

This landscape stimulated Muir to pursue a lifetime of exploring nature and working for the preservation of natural areas.

The Muirs stayed at Fountain Lake until December 1856 when Sarah Muir married David Galloway. They moved to Hickory Hill Farm while the Galloways took over most of the original farm. In 1860 John left home for other pursuits, but March 1864 found him back at Fountain Lake Farm with Sarah and David.

One sunny September day I walked the rustic path around Fountain Lake. I envisioned how it was in May of 1849 when the wagon drawn by ox team lumbered onto the land carrying Daniel Muir, three of his children and their household goods. I could feel eleven-year-old John's excitement when he jumped off the wagon and beheld the scene before him.

From where I sat I pictured the life of the Muir family here almost 150 years ago. Despite hours of toil under the stern father, young John was somehow able to combine his farm work with his love of nature. He closely examined the natural world around him and took advantage of every possible scrap of time to use his creative abilities. I could see him whittling ingenious inventions from shagbark hickory and reading in stolen moments.

An ancient open-grown white oak, its outstretched limbs standing guard as it did when John roamed here. There were no hickory trees from Muir's time but others dotted the woodlands.

When I walked through the old Muir farm I imagined young John working in the fields and taking a moment to enjoy the beauty around him. The farmland contained a sandblow that was almost devoid of plants. A few prairie plants grew there, some scrub oaks, and an occasional earth star.

At the end of my ramble it was a joy to walk through the prairie on the north side of the lake where grasses mingled with colorful flowers.

As I completed the circle of the lake I was impressed yet again with the diversity of the plant communities that made up the landscape Muir explored as a youth. I was pleased to see the fine results of work being done to restore the lands to native species that grew here at the time of settlement. It was a wonderful place for the pioneer ecologist to explore the secrets of nature.

Though John Muir spent many years exploring the Sierra Nevada and other splendid places, he never forgot the land of his youth. It had inspired him to save treasured parts of the national landscape.

As for me, when he once wrote to his Wisconsin family: "You live in one of the most beautiful regions under the sun," he expressed the feeling I have for this region I call mine.

Millie Stanley lives in Marquette County and is the author of The Heart of John Muir's World.

My Island

DENNIS MCCANN

The moment, like most conceits, was largely harmless.

And, like most conceits, so wrongheaded.

One winter's day, as has been sung, in a deep and dark December I stood with my wife on the icy edge of Lake Superior, along a shoreline that stretched out and away like welcoming arms, and we said yes, this is our island, our haven where we have found rest and refreshment on more than a dozen summer stays and now in snowy winter, too.

Lonely, empty winter, when solitude heightens the sense of ownership. What must be shared in summer with sun bathers, black flies and buzzing red scooters — scourges all — is for a moment no one else's, and so it is ours. Our island, our park, our place.

Back in town, the true islanders — hardy souls who stay the winter and work hard to pay the mortgage — deserve to harrumph. And a few miles away in the island's snow-covered Indian cemetery, next to the fancy marina but across chilly Chequamegon Bay from the reservation where his people were moved a century ago, the spirit of old Chief Buffalo must have stirred in wry amusement.

There was a man who understood how ephemeral is ownership.

We don't own Madeline Island, my wife and I, and it might surprise the army of Jeep-driving Minnesotans who are building summer homes that will never be mistaken for cottages, but they don't own it, either.

That's not how it works. The island, with its soul-tugging wonders, owns us. I know it owns me.

It is easy to say that Bayfield and the Apostle Islands are what Door County used to be before it became the Dells, and what the Dells used to be before that. Rugged as a leading man, as alluring as his lady. And every year more and more visitors reach the same conclusion that the far-off northern tip of Wisconsin has not yet been despoiled by water parks and condominiums that tax the resource and the visitor, too. It is so obvious that when a Chicago writer searched for the Midwest's finest small town and awarded the crown to Bayfield and the Apostles, few were surprised.

But if the merchants were ecstatic, as the boastful t-shirts rushed into their windows seemed to say, the ferry-catcher in me was dismayed. How long will the line be this year?

To my island.

There it is again.

I think of the change I have seen in 15 years of island hopping and I worry. I think of the change that has been visited on Madeline in 15,000 years, since the receding fingers of the last glacier carved that barrier beach where I stood alone in winter, and worry a little bit less. People will always seek it out, as the Chippewa and the fur traders and the lumberers did before the sailors took their turn, but Madeline's defense against Doordom will always be its very identity, a long spit of land in the midst of a muscled and often inhospitable great lake.

It keeps out the riff-raff — in February, anyway. But in July when the crowds come with firecrackers, and in October when the apples ripen and the end of autumn is toasted with cider all around, Bayfield and the Apostles have all they can handle. Good for the merchants, good for the local folks who serve the food and pour the drinks and change the beds, and good for me because I need them like they need me. Isn't that they way it always goes? I'm the answer, and I'm the problem.

I own not an acre but I own it all, and so I worry. Change creeps in like shadows, but shadows are chased by the light of day while change just is. The island owns us all, at its peril.

Dennis McCann writes for the Milwaukee Journal Sentinel.

Seeking Sauk Prairie

CURT MEINE

In the old days, according to August Derleth, it would have been easier to unearth a herd of unicorns than unity on the Sauk Prairie. But time, like the bark of a fire-scarred prairie oak, has overgrown the old wounds. Although the towns have resisted legal unification, more and more of the local business, institutions, and billboards have adopted the area's umbrella designation of "Sauk Prairie."

The shift in terminology is fitting, I think, and holds a hidden promise. The two town names are certainly evocative. Officially chartered, adopted, and platted, they carry political authority. But Sauk Prairie was and is a place. The promise is that politics may come to be understood within a sense of place.

Continuity is necessary because change is constant. And as the pace of cultural change has accelerated, the need for continuity has grown increasingly important — and desperate. Community institutions that have traditionally provided a degree of continuity now face the challenge of keeping pace. What does our contemporary longing to strengthen our families and communities represent but a concerted effort to weave at one end of the social fabric what rapid economic and technological change are fraying at the other? Until recently, however, discussions of continuity have rarely included the landscape in which our communities are embedded. Can there be any continuity if the very sources and setting of our communities are left out of the picture?

Sauk Prairie will not be alone in confronting such questions. And it has that name, which makes it difficult to ignore its origins in Indian country and in tallgrass prairie. In Sauk Prairie, as elsewhere, much of the past and of the natural has been obliterated; but much still is on display.

Sauk Prairie sits in a bowl. The rims consist of pre-Cambrian quartzite in the Baraboo Range to the north, ridges of Ordovician sandstone to the west, and the Wisconsin River with its associated bluffs to the east and south. The gentle ridge of the terminal moraine bisects the bowl; to its west is outwash plain, to its east rolling hills and pothole ponds. Some combination of topography, local soil type, prevailing winds, rainfall patterns, fire, grazing animals, and the activities of native people allowed the bottom of the bowl to support at the time of European contact a 14,000-acre expanse of prairie, grading along its edges into oak savanna and woodland.

The Sauk Prairie proper stretched south from the base of the bluffs, then west to meet the sandstone. As with so many early descriptions of the midwest's tallgrass empire, the accounts of Sauk Prairie's explorers and settlers often waxed rhapsodic. One noted the "myriad of flowers of every shape, shade and color, and the luxuriant grasses.... a handsome picture set in a beautiful frame..." The perceptive modern traveler along US Highway 12 can read where the prairie lay.

For the first travelers along the lower Wisconsin, Sauk Prairie must also have done wonders for perspective. Whether Ho Chunk, Sauk, or Fox, or the later missionaries, trappers, and explorers, they gained at Sauk Prairie a glimpse between worlds. Descending the river from the Fox-Wisconsin portage just upstream, travelers would here have come upon the first open expanse of prairie along the water route west, a first hint of the mid-continent's great grasslands. Conversely, ascending the river from the Mississippi below, they would have left the prairie behind them here, adjusting their eyes from grasses to forests, and their bellies from bison to deer. At Sauk Prairie, they gave continuity to the divided biomes of what is now Wisconsin.

Sauk Prairie has a history as contested territory. The fundamental scrape, between the ice and the earth, left us the moraine and the outwash and Devil's Lake nearby. Through twelve subsequent millennia, forest, oak savanna, and prairie skirmished for control. The shape and extent of Sauk Prairie changed with the ages, expanding with aridity, shrinking with moisture. Burr oaks, which Aldo Leopold described as "the shock troops sent by the invading forest to storm the prairie," shifted position in response to the frequency of fire and the abundance of rain. Oak openings thinned and thickened with the changing conditions.

The prairie gained its name from the native Sauk who made it their home place prior to European contact, coexisting with the nearby Ho Chunk. First pushed west by the territorial expansions of eastern tribes, then relocated beyond the Mississippi by the incoming Europeans, the Sauk left only their name. In 1832 Black Hawk's desperate Sauk band returned from exile and sought to reestablish continuity with the land. They barely saved themselves through their heroic resistance at Black Hawk Ridge, which rises above the Wisconsin River at the south edge of the prairie. Days later, their own continuity was all but lost on the Bad Axe.

Then followed the continuing disputes between the immigrant villages on the prairie's fringe. Subsequent bouts featured a clash over where to bridge the river, a "thunderous rift" in Sauk City's Roman Catholic congregation, and an argument about placement of Highway 12 through town. Meanwhile, outside of town, plows overturned the prairie sod, and the struggle to extract organic wealth commenced. Early rounds, involving wheat and chinch bugs, hops and hop-borers, passed quickly before the search for a more sustainable agriculture began. By the late 1800s the farms had diversified, the mix of livestock and grains mimicking the pre-agricultural mix of the grazers and the grazed.

And then the global forces and local landscape collided, abruptly and unpredictably, in the Sauk Prairie. Even before the United States entered World War II, plans to build an ammunitions manufacturing facility in the area had taken shape. With the assault on Pearl Harbor, events progressed inexorably. Occupying much of the northern half of the former Sauk Prairie, built through the swift and bitter removal of some eighty farm families, the Badger Ordnance Works (later renamed the Badger Army Ammunition Plant) went from paper plans to production in little more than a year.

The Badger Army Ammunition Plant is now closing, a poignant end to this disputatious century — and with closure, another contest has begun: to determine the fate of the plant's 7,453 acres and, in a way, of the natural and human history that lies dormant in its soil. Again the continuity of prairie and oak savanna, of the native presence, of the farmer's efforts, and of commerce and industry are in question. The outcome will display to all, and to posterity, our capacity to learn and respect our history; to define and locate our community within the broader landscape; to create a necessary continuity not out of desperation, but out of an awareness of needs, responsibilities, and possibilities.

Passing regularly through the Sauk Prairie in the late 1930s and 1940s, Aldo Leopold observed the gradual diminution of the roadside prairie remnants, the removal of the farm families, the construction of the ordnance works. It is said that the experimental efforts in ecological restoration that Leopold helped initiate at the University of Wisconsin's arboretum involved, in part, genetic stock from prairie species in the river bluffs overlooking Sauk Prairie. Continuity was much on his mind, and those of other conservationists, in those years. The durability of the midwest's prairie soils, of the continent's wild places, and even, during and after the war, of the human enterprise itself, was in question. Leopold framed the issue, inimitably, through the eyes of a prairie dweller. Reflecting upon the elimination of Sauk Prairie's native flora and fauna, he wrote, "What a thousand acres of Silphiums looked like when they tickled the bellies of the buffalo is a question never again to be answered, and perhaps not even asked." His fear was well justified, but perhaps his despair premature. Many in Sauk Prairie are asking such questions again, and seeking answers.

Often on still winter mornings at Sauk Prairie, thin veils of mist rise up off the Wisconsin River and drift over the valley's brim. The layered wisps hang like pieces of a delicate mobile, mingling with woodsmoke rising from the chimneys of town homes and farm houses. Morning sunlight angles in over the river bluffs, sometimes carrying shadows of the bald eagles that ply river and sky through the winter months. The river, freed from its last dam upstream of Prairie du Sac, slides west toward its meeting with the Mississippi. On the coldest mornings, all things in sight, from the river to the Baraboo Hills, grow crystals of frozen fog. Of all the moods of the Sauk Prairie landscape, this is the one I find most settling. The stories of this place, layered like the fog, lift and drift and mingle. We see through time in patches, we are struck by light, shadows of the other creatures cross us. We are connected, and try to arrange for continuity.

Curt Meine is a conservation biologist for the International Crane Foundation in Baraboo. He is also the author of the book, The Biography of Aldo Leopold: His Life and Work.

Suspended Animation

MARY SCHAFER

I had known it when I looked out the window last evening at the fading sunlight. The last orange rays were streaking and bouncing off clouds moving in from the west, gunmetal gray and lowering. Against the pale snow already on the ground, the approaching storm looked darker and even more ominous than usual. I descended into the cellar to toss another log in the furnace. It was a deed of resignation as, only midway through October, I reconciled myself with the thought of another early winter at my Wisconsin home north of the 45th parallel.

Sure enough, I awoke this morning to a new mantle of white that had fallen while I slept. The windows were veiled with condensation on the lower half of the panes, and I peered through the top half to watch the last, almost insignificant flakes of the lingering storm drift to the ground.

After breakfast, I went out to the porch and pulled the wide janitorial broom from its place in the corner. Pushing the porch door till it creaked open, I realized how much that lonesome sound made the day seem much colder than the 20 degrees it actually was. My two dogs dashed madly out the opening for their first breath of crisp, morning air. For them, Labrador retrievers with winter coats already thickened, it was rarely too cold, too early.

The broom handle clacked against the drip edging as I scraped the fluff from the edges of the roof, trying to avoid the damaging ice dams of last year. The rhythmic "thump, ssssssh.., thump, ssssssh" of my work was interrupted by a whirring past my head, I turned to watch a tiny popcorn ball of a chickadee land, cock his head and scuttle-about on the feeder. A red-breasted nuthatch perched comically on the edge, his rump in the air as he slashed his head from side to side in the piles of shell detritus, scattering black blotches about the base of the feeder in search of a striped seed that hadn't yet been looted.

By this time, the dogs were anxious to get going on their morning constitutional, so we started down the drive to the road, which was discernible only as a slightly grayer ribbon slicing the expanse of white on either side. Gone were the bright patches of orange and yellow that had quilted the ground beneath the maples and aspens just days before. Now, the needlely green fingers of the red pines and spruce stretched outward and upward, catching piles of the frothy white that tumbled from the sky.

We ambled down the road, me inhaling great lungsful of the biting air, the dogs burying their noses with myriad scents known only to them. I glanced across a field to the small pond that lay at the bottom of our tamarack bog. Sheets of ice had formed and were turning to white rafts on the dark water, which was reflecting the greenblack of the surrounding balsams. The water lay still, no ripples marring its smooth surface as it awaited the shell of imperfect glass that would soon encase it in suspended animation.

The dogs were now through with their serious business and turned to play. They flipped over sideways in the snow, packing down icy runways as they slid happily along its coldness, propelled by the windmill motions of their muscular legs. They sneezed and snorted as the crystals found their way into wide, wet nostrils. Suddenly, some sound in the distance interrupted their frolicking, and they leapt to their feet, legs braced and heads turned, motionless.

Their bodies created a picturesque composition, as black and sharp against the bright white background as the antique cut-paper silhouettes I had found in my grandmother's photo album. A touch of cheer was added to the scene by the arrival of a pair of cardinals, the male alighting on a drooping hemlock limb, looking for all the world like a bright red ornament. Whatever had made the sound was gone as quickly as it had come, for the two lost interest and dropped their heads back to the frozen ground beneath them, sniffing and snooping, poking their noses deep into the snow.

Having enjoyed our fill of the snowy morning, we made our way slowly back to the house, a small blue box nestled between tall white birch and dark maples. A wispy film of smoke curled lazily from the chimney, beckoning me back to its promise of warmth. Despite what the calendar on the kitchen wall said, I could feel the hands on my inner clock shift into deep winter time, turning more slowly and without relativity to anything but the cycles of thinly lit days and clear, velour nights.

Mary Shafer is a writer, illustrator, adventurer, and author of the book, Wisconsin: The Way We Were.

Honey Creek

HAROLD KRUSE

My own personal "discovery" of the Honey Creek Valley, also known as Born's Valley or Indian Trail Valley, happened in the mid-1940s. During and after high school days, it was my custom to spend Sunday afternoons on long rambles over the countryside, with our farm dog for a companion, exploring woodland and meadow and all the fascinating nooks and crannies of the natural landscape.

On the most memorable of those treks, we had been walking for hours down a wooded ravine when we suddenly found ourselves on an open hogsback ridge, overlooking a splendid panorama — a meandering stream bordered by hemlock-covered cliffs over-topped by steep wooded hillsides extending into the distance. The valley then, as now, was rich in ferns and wildflower, with birdsong everywhere. That afternoon of exploration and discovery left me with a deep resolve to do whatever it might take to protect this treasure trove of natural beauty for the future.

The opportunity for action came in 1956, when I had the pleasure of leading a group of kindred spirits down the Honey Creek Valley on the first of what were to become annual treks. It was a delightful June day, blue phlox carpeted the valley, goldfinches were everywhere, and sightings of Kentucky warbler, scarlet tanager, gnatcatcher, and a host of other common and uncommon birds left indelible impressions on the minds of the trekkers. The trip led directly to a decision a year later by the Wisconsin Society for Ornithology (WSO) to establish a nature preserve at Honey Creek.

Honey Creek Valley, westernmost of the many rocky gorges and valleys of the Baraboo Range, is unique in its great diversity of habitat and plant and animal life. Of the 25 plant communities in the Baraboo Hills, over one-third occur at Honey Creek: stream and open water, cattail marsh and sedge meadow, alder bog and shrub carr, tamarack, white pine and hardwood swamp, lowland and upland hardwoods, hemlock cliffs and white pine, open cliff and high, dry "goat prairies." More than 500 native plant species have been identified, including 20 varieties of ferns, several orchids and the endangered bog bluegrass.

However interesting the plants may be, birds are what the Honey Creek Valley is really all about. From tiny hummingbird and sprightly gnatcatcher to soaring vulture and stately sandhill crane, birds of all colors, sizes, shapes and melodic-abilities inhabit the valley and adjoining wetlands. The warm southerly exposure and broad variety of habitats attract an equally broad variety of nesting birds. Through the past 35 years, more than 100 species have been recorded during the nesting season, including a dozen different wood warblers.

Along the creek one may see wood duck and mallard, green and great blue heron (the great blues have a rookery in the tallest tree atop the valley's highest hill), eastern phoebe, belted kingfisher and northern rough-winged swallow. In the bogs and marshes are sandhill crane, American woodcock, common snipe, rails, swamp sparrow, and corn on yellow-throat and yellow warblers, while extensive edge habitat harbors gray catbird, rose-breasted grosbeak, northern cardinal, eastern bluebird, indigo bunting, song sparrow, and blue-winged warbler.

Woodpeckers, including the pileated, range throughout the Honey Creek valley, as do the other permanent residents: American crow, bluejay, black-capped chickadee, white-breasted nuthatch, ruffed grouse, red-tailed hawk and wild turkey. Veerys nest in the tamarack bog, and also in the deep woods, where their companions are the wood thrush, scarlet tanager, redeyed vireo, Kentucky and cerulean warblers, American redstart and barred owl. The creek's banks are home to Louisiana water thrush, the hemlocks to Acadian flycatcher, and the drier upland hardwoods to whippoorwill.

Killdeers frequent Honey Creek Valley's remaining open pasture lands, but the grazing cattle also attract the parasitic cowbird, bane of forest songbirds. The cowbird builds no nest of its own but lays its eggs in the nests of warblers, flycatchers, wood thrush and others, where soon, the fast growing cowbird young crowd out and outcompete the host species' own young for food and attention. As ecologists have recently learned in the Baraboo Hills and elsewhere, large unbroken tracts of woodland offer the only real protection against this pest.

For an unforgettable experience, come to Honey Creek some calm June morning before sunrise to hear the dawn chorus. The first hint of light in the eastern sky brings forth a few tentative notes by catbird or song sparrow, and the chorus gradually swells until, come sunrise, it is difficult to separate one birdsong from another. By midmorning many of the musicians have stopped singing and have gone about their insect gathering and other business of the day. By noon, especially on hot days, only vireos and indigo buntings may still be singing, but toward evening the chorus swells again.

* * *

The Honey Creek reserve was established with three main purposes in mind. First and foremost, to ensure a continued healthy and adequate environment and habitat for the many plants and wild "critters" calling the valley home. Secondly, to provide recreation — birding, botany, hiking, photography — for Wisconsin Society for Ornithology (WSO) members and friends, including all who share an appreciation for "things natural, wild and free." And lastly, to encourage scientific study and conservation education activities.

Whatever may be the future uses for the Honey Creek Natural Area, we need to exercise restraint and caution. At what point does use become overuse? When does management turn into overmanagement? The human urge to "manage" and "improve on" nature is a strong one, but in each case we need to carefully consider whether our actions will bring about the best results, or if it is wiser to let nature take its course and accept whatever comes of it. In any event, the Honey Creek Valley, having gone through many years of grazing and logging, is now largely protected. Barring some natural catastrophe or pollution from human activities, the valley should remain a thing of beauty and a safe haven for its many plant and animal residents well into the future.

Harold Kruse is a farmer, amateur naturalist, and conservationist.

Slanting North

JOHN BATES

A hunger lingers in all of us to live in the natural world. We need to watch eagles take flight from high pines, to hear the wild sounds of cranes from secluded marshes, to smell pungent balsam needles in a dense woodland, to breathe clean sharp air that flares the nostrils. Our affinity for the natural world is why we fill our homes with plants, keep dogs and cats as members of our family (royalty more often than not), and escape the urban world to rural landscapes as often as possible. As a species, our hearts and minds were once necessarily calibrated to natural stimuli, cycles and events. Today our daily survival no longer depends on listening to those internal meters. Still, the meters come unstuck often enough to make us feel that we are missing something, and that until we find it, we won't be whole. It is that innate force within us that draws us upnorth.

How do we define "upnorth"? Upnorth is conveyed by both the presence of wildness and the absence of much of what represents urban life. Maybe it's most easily symbolized by one of the first actions many people take when they come upnorth — they open all the windows (hopefully there are screens to keep the mosquito hordes at bay.) In the city, we work overtime to drive the unnatural sounds and smells away. We close our windows, turn up the radio, the stereo, the TV - we try not to hear or smell. The opposite is true upnorth. One of the great pleasures in April at our home in Manitowish is the opening of windows to let in birdsong, fresh air, and smells of warming soil. The windows close only for storms, nights too cold, and October. If we aren't outside, we try to bring its gifts all in.

And the gifts are many: wood frogs softly quacking on the first warm nights of spring, the voiceless wind translated into genres of music by thrumming pines or rain — like trembling aspen leaves, the holy wailing of loons, the sweet fragrance of trailing arbutus on the heels of receding snow, the pungency of sweet fern on hot days in open pine woods, the blackberry stains on hands and mouths that ate more than they collected, the drowsing warmth of backwater bays clothed in water lilies and pickerel-weed. The list runs on.

Upnorth also represents the opportunities of open spaces and public lands. Map lovers labor here in joy. Which river to paddle today? Which path to hike? Which early morning lake to watch as the fogs lift? Which old road to park the car and explore? Which bog to seek orchids? The topo maps beckon and cajole, much like an exotic seed catalog to the urban gardener.

Upnorth is a place to be a part of, to stay in, a home to hang your final hat. I have no need to go anywhere else. The Northwoods is a perpetual present waiting to be opened, if I simply take the time to open myself to it. That means that while the Northwoods can be pointed to on a map, it is also a state of mind. Unless you bring to it a quiet respect and a desire for honest membership, you may be bored with the quiet, the lack of "things to do." Travel here is both inward and outward. Those who forget the inward component spend their days on things like jetskis circling, circling, circling... Herein lays the great challenge. Can we learn to be a simple member of the northern community, or will we impose our wills so dramatically on the landscape that we end up destroying the peace and beauty for which we first came?

It's an old story of course, played out worldwide for as long as we can remember, and probably into the future for as long as we can imagine. The curses have gathered: the sprawl, the shoreline development, the mines, the concept that the North Country can be all things for all people, a recreational playground that accommodates whatever our human drives can create. Look carefully at the scenes in the Northwoods that speak most deeply to you. They are visions that speak as much to what is there as to what isn't. The captions to them could easily read, "This is a river that doesn't have a mill on it." "This is a lake where sunrises come up over trees, not homes." "This is the Northwoods, not the Northlawns." Proponents of escalated development speak disdainfully of NIMBY's — "Not In My Backyard" conservationists. I'm proud to be a NIMBY. This backyard is worth saving exactly as it is.

But enough talk. The Manitowish River is calling. A harrier has flown upriver. Snipe are winnowing over the marshes. A bittern is pumper-lunking from somewhere below the house. It's time to try again to find my place in it all.

John Bates writes for Manitowish River Press, *freelances, and writes books. An earlier version of this essay appeared in* Wisconsin Trails *(July 1997). John recently published* A Northwoods Campaign: Spring and Summer.

A Sense of Place

NINA LEOPOLD BRADLEY

I write of my own attachment to a particular place. It happened over time with my family, on a sand farm along the Wisconsin River — land that was neither grand nor dramatic, but mundane, humbled, and degraded. It seems to have happened by slow accrual. I dwell in, and am finally a part of this place.

Recently I came across a splendid little book by Deborah Tall, who inspired me with the following statement: "How does land evoke our love? Surely not just driving through scenery or landscape, treating nature as a prop."

It seems all too often we hurry through "scenery" without any attempt to engage the land, the price we pay for our mobility and rootlessness.

On our sand farm along the Wisconsin River I was able to get inside the scenery and the landscape. As we worked with family, friends and neighbors to restore the abused land, we were experiencing the sensitizing of people to land. We learned how to look at, how to dwell on and how to think about land.

In "A Sand County Almanac" Father wrote: "My own farm was selected for its lack of goodness and its lack of highway. In fact my whole farm lies in the backwash of the River Progress."

Gross understatement. The sandy soils, outwash from the glacier, had produced one or two crops of corn — perhaps a crop of buckwheat or rye before the soils were exhausted. Any timber had been cut. The corned out fields were coming up in sand burs and quack grass. Sand burrs in our socks were effective reminders.

There was little left to support a farm family. The previous owner had finally given up and moved to California, the farm house having burned to the ground. The only remaining structure was an old chicken coop, waist deep in chicken and cow manure.

What could be more of a challenge for a bunch of teenagers than repairing the chicken coop. Weekend after weekend, the Leopold family worked to make the chicken coop more habitable - cleaning out manure, constructing a fireplace, attaching a bunk house, a new roof, driving a small sand-point well, and many other items contributing to comfort.

The "Shack" became a family enterprise to which each member contributed: cutting and splitting wood, building bird houses for martins, screech owls and bluebirds.

In my father's quiet way we finally were led to understand his direction: what did this land look like before white man took it away from the Indians. Reconstruction of the native landscape became our aim. We now realize this was one of the earliest attempts at ecological restoration.

From April to October scarcely a weekend went by that someone did not plant or transplant something — butterfly weed, tamarack, wahoo and oak, penstemon and puccoon. Spring vacation became the principal planting season. Each year we planted some 3,000 pines, planted them with shovels so sharp they sang and hummed in our wrists as they sliced the earth. We planted a mosaic of conifers, hardwoods and prairie to restore health and beauty to the community.

In winter we banded resident birds. We recorded daily, weekly, seasonal events on the land — tracks of animals in the snow, arrival of migratory geese, courtship of woodcock, etc. Here in reality Father's statement rang true "keeping records enhances the pleasure of the search, and the chance of finding order and meaning in these events."

It was our mother whose enthusiasm sustained the project. Mother worked as hard as anyone, planting, weeding, she was "chief sawyer" as the gang cut good oak to cook our grub and warm our Shack.

With mother's Spanish background she taught us Spanish songs and each evening the guitar concert filled the shack until weariness forced us to our bunks.

In years of drought, our struggling plantings did not survive. We learned that "sun, wind and rain" and the thrust of life determine the outcome of our investment in the place.

Here in the sand counties, Aldo Leopold initiated a different relationship with the land, at once more personal and more universal. From his direct participation in the land he was to come to a deeper appreciation of the ecological, ethical, and aesthetic understanding and at the same time finding new dimension to his sense of place.

What happened involved the senses, the memory, the history of family. It came from working on the land in all weathers, suffering from catastrophes, enjoying its mornings or evenings or hot noons, valuing it for the investment of labor and feeling.

By his actions my father instilled in his children a love and respect for the land community and its ecological functioning.

"There are two things that interest me — the relationship of people to each other and the relationship of people to land."

Family weekends at our sand farm were to be the place where my father put these two concepts into practice: the relationship of our family members to each other, and to this piece of land.

At the Shack, we all became participants in the land's workings. In the very process of restoration — of planting, of successes and failures, of animals and birds responding to changes — we grew to appreciate the interconnectedness of living systems.

As we transformed the land, it transformed us; this is how a sense of place is nurtured. My father once wrote that restoration can be a ritual of self renewal, and so it was.

One of the principal achievements of "A Sand County Almanac" is the recasting of our notion of natural beauty, away from the conventionally "scenic" to the more subtle sense that comes with ecological and evolutionary awareness.

Through my father, my family, and this experience, I have learned to love this land. This place taught me how to look, how to live, and at last to sing its poetry.

Nina Leopold Bradley writes as a member of Wisconsin's "first family" of conservation and ecology. She remains active on land use issues.

Struggles

Why?

MAKATAI MESHE KIAKIAK

I had many good memories of our lands. The spirit of a giant swan visited me in a vision in a cave.

We were prosperous in the Rock River country. We had over 800 acres under cultivation. The graves of our ancestors were in that country. We had friends among the Winnebago and Pottawatomi. We fished the rivers, mined the lead, and traveled to Iowa to hunt buffalo.

The settlers came. My son and daughter died of disease. Our young men were murdered. Our crops were destroyed. I was beaten and accused of hog theft.

I loved our fields and gardens, our corn and squash, the rivers and islands, and the places of our ancestors. I fought for them.

Makatai Meshe Kiakiak (Black Sparrow Hawk) is better known as the Sac leader Black Hawk. He was the principal character in the 1832 land use dispute known as the Black Hawk War. The above piece is adapted from his various responses to why he chose to take on the military might of the United States to resist removal.

A Letter to Aldo Leopold

April 21, 1998

Dear Aldo:

Change is a constant in our world. Almost daily the destructive forces of nature blow, flood, flame, or shake some portion of our planet. But places where people live and places which people love can be changed as dramatically — if not always as swiftly — by the actions of mankind.

Of course, I need not remind you of this. For it was you, Aldo, who chronicled changes wrought by the forces of nature on that sand-blown farm you loved. Maybe you are not amazed at what a different place your riverside retreat is today compared to what it was like in 1935, but I am. Walking to or from the Shack, it is difficult for me to comprehend this is the same parcel of land as pictured on those black and white photographs Nina exhibits to those who visit the Reserve.

Our landscape is much changed from what it was during your residency. If that "good oak" of yours was still putting on annual rings, it now would have recorded other milestones in the natural resources history of our state — some of which, I imagine, would elicit a satisfying nod of your head but others surely would furrow your brow.

The wild ones are back—both predators and prey. Wolves in our state numbered in the thousands in the 1850s. Over the next one hundred years, the "fierce green fire" that had raged in the eyes of these majestics had been completely snuffed out. In recent years, wolves from remote places in Minnesota have been migrating into our state on their own. The present-day population of wolves is estimated at 150 and it continues to grow.

Another welcomed wildlife reintroduction is the wild turkey, which disappeared from our state just after the Civil War. Turkeys brought from Missouri now have multiplied and spread into more than half the state's counties. Hunters harvested twenty thousand of these wily birds during the past season leaving at least ten times as many in the wild.

A creature you feared was on the edge of extinction, Aldo, has made a dramatic comeback. You reported that probably no more than twenty pairs of sandhill cranes were to be found in Wisconsin in the 1920s. Today, the estimated summer population of adult sandhills is 2900 pairs.

The population of bald eagles — once nearly wiped out of our state because of reproduction problems owing to pesticide in their food sources — has rebounded. Today we have an estimated 645 nesting pairs. It is not uncommon to see 100 eagles at one time at prime viewing spots along the Wisconsin River.

Again we can hear the glorious call of trumpeter swans in Wisconsin. Restoration begun a few years back has a goal of twenty nesting pairs by the end of the century. Unfortunately, there have been setbacks. Imprudent hunters have shot several of these birds whose wingspan exceeds the width of my outstretched arms. In most cases, they said they mistook a swan for the smaller snow goose.

There is both good news and bad news concerning wetlands. Half the state's original wetland has been drained or filled. Frogs have decreased in number and more specimens are exhibiting limb deformities. Similar problems are apparent in the state's salamander population. It is probably safe to speculate that less visible aquatic organisms also are suffering from habitat destruction. Yet wetlands, more and more, are being recognized for their system value.

Near the city of Montello, I am pleased to report, a group of landowners led by Vincent Metcalf have been restoring about three square miles of drained land that once produced bounties of carrots, lettuce, and mint. Easements have been purchased thus assuring this wetland will be undisturbed in the future. With the technical help of the U.S. Fish and Wildlife Service, this area has become home to furred, finned, and feathered creatures that favor such habitat. Humans will benefit too because the marsh collects eroded silt, utilizes nutrients dissolved in the water, and reduces flood potential.

Only five hundred (of five million) acres of oak savanna existing in our state during presettlement times are intact. And few original tracts of pine exist. Some reports suggest only 250 prairie acres remain. Efforts are being made to protect these remnants.

The most alarming statistic, Aldo, does not concern eagles, frogs, oak savannas, wetlands, or prairies. The most startling numbers are about us — the humans that call Wisconsin home. While there need be no alarm sounded about declining numbers, perhaps a red flag should be waved for the opposite reason. Human activity is affecting our state at the expense of native plants and animals, farm fields, woodlots, scenic vistas, and quiet waterways.

Farmland is being converted for urban/suburban uses at a monumental pace. Within my lifetime, eight million acres disappeared mostly under asphalt, concrete, roofs, and manicured lawns. Sprawl not only adversely affects farmland but also the wooded portions of our state.

Undeveloped shoreline has become a scarce commodity in our state. Humans are rapidly occupying the perimeters of lakes and the banks of streams where native biota formerly thrived. The result is an environmental "Catch 22." The components of the natural world that attracted people to these settings (clean water, abundant wildlife, shade trees, and restful quiet) are being degraded.

Sprawl may get even worse because Wisconsin needs to find a place for 400,000 additional households in the next twenty years. Where should we put these people, Aldo? Until the present time, we have done a poor job of deciding which areas should be developed and which ones should not. Our state does not have a well-conceived or widely accepted land use vision. Policies are needed to retain our state's distinctive rural character, to maintain its regions of natural and cultural diversity, and to effectively accommodate expected growth in areas for which this growth is best suited.

State and local leaders must set land use goals for the future; that is, they need to develop a coherent, deliberate, and proactive growth management strategy. As 1000 Friends of Wisconsin — a new statewide group of citizens interested in responsible land use—has advocated, we need to set measurable (not mushy) benchmarks for various uses of land in our state. For instance, in the year 2020, we should still be farming ninety-five percent of the most agriculturally productive soils that were being farmed in 1995. Similarly, we should retain undeveloped shoreline not less than ninety percent of the shoreline area that existed in 1995. Knowing what it is we want to accomplish (ends) will save us the trouble of applying land use management techniques (means) that are destined to fail.

Aldo, effective land use management in Wisconsin is grounded in your philosophy of land. Few have grasped that humans are to "live by and with rather than merely on the land." Possessors of land are more than owners. We are more than custodians. We are components of a landscape with which we must interact harmoniously not competitively.

As I write, Aldo, it is exactly fifty years since that small fire erupted on your neighbor's land. Your determination to extinguish that fire led to your passing. However, the great fire of your ideas of mankind and the land have ever since burned.

May this forever be so.

Your Admiring Friend,
Don

Don Last is a professor in the UW-Stevens Point College of Natural Resources and editor of Law of the Land Review.

Woodchuck Bonanza

JIM CHIZEK

In the 1940's the area around Fifield was interspersed with small subsistence farms, where once regal pine forests and Indians reigned. The dull thump of dynamite was commonly heard as farmers sweated and toiled to clear and enlarge their holdings among the thousands of giant pine stumps remaining from the pine cut of the middle 1800s. As the stumps were pried, chopped and pulled from the ground an unholy crop of rocks of all sizes remained.

As mechanization replaced horse power, farmers began to use bulldozers to push the debris into windrows of stumps and rocks mixed with dirt and tangled brush along side each clearing. Farm after farm had these windrows. They became ideal habitat for woodchucks. As their populations exploded, not a garden or field crop was safe as the multitude of voracious rodents dined royally.

All out war broke out as farmers valiantly fought a losing battle with guns, traps and dogs to save crops they so depended on during the last pangs of the Great Depression. But as every conservationist knows, until the environment is changed, man cannot prevail.

While traps were an effective way to control pests, not many were used for fear of catching prize chuck dogs. These dogs were allowed to run loose so they could constantly hunt and kill woodchucks. A good chuck dog was thought to be sent from heaven. His character must be a dog of a mixed breed, sturdy enough to withstand a woodchuck's stamina and determination in a fight to the death. He must be fast enough to catch them in their mad dash for their burrow. He must possess the courage of a lion to press into the fray in spite of the woodchuck's pugnacity. Once aroused chucks give no quarter, given the chance to retreat to their burrow they choose to fight viciously to their death.

At his mother's insistence Jim set a trap in a woodchuck borrow in the corner of their garden in an attempt to save the tender shoots emerging from the ground. His 13 year-old sister Etta insisted on accompanying him during this operation. Put off by big brother, she was prone to investigate. Suddenly there was a terrified shriek at the burrow. Jim ran to his sister who was sitting near the burrow crying and staring at the number 1 trap clamped on her hand. Quickly he grasped and sprung the trap, releasing her.

Picking up the trap Jim and Etta were heading toward their house when intercepted by their mother. "Jimmy you get back out there and set that trap. I want those woodchucks killed before they clean out my garden."

"But Ma, Etta already got caught in it and I'm afraid old Teddy will get caught in it too — He's always after woodchucks."

"Listen to me young man, I want those creatures out of my garden. Now set the trap and lock the dog up. Etta you stay away from that trap." The trap did catch several chucks who were soon replaced by others.

The stage was set in the spring of 1945 for strange events to follow as result of a competition between 15 year old Jim and Earl, his 25 year old neighbor. Bragging of their prowess as woodchuck hunters, a challenge was raised as to who could kill the most chucks before freeze up. Chucks trapped or dogged were not be counted.

Jim had a slight advantage as he knew of a large stump that must have been cut during a winter with very deep snow. The 6-foot stump towered about 8 feet from the ground near where his uncle had planted a large garden. A woodchuck haven! Approximately 30 burrows had been dug around its outstretched giant roots. As chucks were killed others moved in.

Barefoot as the other young lads of that time, Jim lugged his single shot .22 rifle everywhere he went that entire summer. Often he lay in wait for hours for a chuck to venture far enough from his den to make a killing head shot. Even a slightly imperfect hit would send the animal running into the burrow to die. A no counter! Besides he had no money to replace the shells he used. Using shorts, the cheapest he could buy, he had to make every shot count.

The toll continued to rise with the count of each reaching near 20 at the end of June.

Noticing Earl each morning, rifle in hand, sneak hunt his way to his mailbox which was several hundred yards from Jim's home, gave him an idea of how this daily habit could be used to trick him.

Chuckling, carrying a freshly killed woodchuck, Jim deftly propped the animal up with sticks in a sitting position they often took, near Earl's mailbox. Arranging some freshly dug dirt in a pile, near the dead animal he simulated a freshly dug woodchuck hole. Carefully inspecting his handiwork he left satisfied the animal partially hidden behind some small hazelnut brush would be visible and realistic enough to fool Earl's trained eye.

As the mail was delivered the following morning Jim waited expectantly in a spruce clump near the sitting woodchuck. He watched intently as Earl slowly hunted his way along the dirt road. Carefully he placed each step so as to not displace or roll a pebble or crunch the gravel, eyes constantly roving so as to not to miss a furtive movement in the brush covered roadside.

Admiring his stealthy approach, Jim mused he's a good hunter, don't miss a thing, hope he don't miss my ambush! Reaching the decoy Earl suddenly stopped and peered intently through the short brush. Jerking the rifle to his shoulder he carefully aimed and fired. Struggling to fit another shell into the single shot 22, he squatted as Jim was greeted by several more shots, each time the struggle between shots becoming more frenzied as he became more desperate in loading.

Choking on guffaw, Jim controlled himself long enough to see what would transpire next. Close enough to see Earl's reaction, Jim was delighted as Earl's face clouded with the realization of what had transpired. Quickly he glanced from side to side, 'wonder if anyone saw me.' His jaw dropped as Jim came slipping from hiding.

"Hi Earl, get him?"

"Damn you, you set this up."

"Wouldn't deny it and wasn't it fine! In fact I just came down to make sure you add this one to my count. By the way how long did you think that chuck was going to sit there and let you shoot at him? Ha Ha."

Jim gleefully spread the story throughout the neighborhood. Earl had shot a dead woodchuck.

Jim Chizek is the author of Game Warden Centurion. *He is a retired Wisconsin DNR conservation warden.*

Land Talk

PAUL GILK

My father and I had a talk, and we weren't exactly the talking types.

He said the farm could barely support one family, and then only if that family were frugal. That was probably in 1975. He was sixty-three years old, had last been a lumberjack in the Rib Lake logging camp days, a trapper and, coming from a big, poor Depression family, a talented out-of-season hunter. He milked slightly over a dozen cows in a barn whose lumber had once been rampikes in burned-over swamps. He had an old Farmall C tractor with single-bottom reversible plows, and he shovelled the gutters by hand rolling the loads by wheelbarrow to the manure pile out back, no matter what the weather. He had cleared every field and had set or driven every fencepost. He was, in his own big-handed way, lord of a little kingdom.

I was just back from nearly ten years in St. Louis, with no degree, no money, a broken marriage, two absent children, and urban burnout. I know what you're saying, I said, I know where you're coming from, but you're totally wrong. There are easily a half-dozen places to build houses on this farm — 120 acres, mostly surrounded by woods — largely out of sight of each other, and the amount of rough pasture that would be disturbed by these little houses and wiggly driveways isn't a fart in a mitten. I ticked off the building sites, one by one. In fact, I went on, if some folks worked off the farm and brought their income back, and we made a fair formula for sharing and distribution, the rest of us could make this place sing. Huge gardens, an orchard, ponds, a saw mill, wind and solar energy, a smokehouse, a market garden, a real working-farm bed-and-breakfast with horse-and-buggy rides and crosscountry ski trails; and, more importantly from a farmer's point of view, we could back off this constant push to maximize production, we could learn the true carrying capacity of the farm, and we could forget the fertilizers and chemicals. The soil would be fat, the critters sleek, nobody would have to work seven days a week, and we could have ourselves a bona fide farm community and be setting a fine example for how rural culture might be revitalized.

He didn't say goddam hippie bullshit, but his face did. I waited. The thing about my father is, no matter what his initial reaction, it's a given that he's gonna look at the thing from your point of view. Well, it's even more than that. He's gonna get inside those thoughts in exactly his own way and try them on for size. So I waited. And pretty soon, sure enough, his face began to change landscape. In his mind he was going to each of those special places where a cabin or cottage or little house would sit. He saw where they'd be sited, how they'd be tucked into the little ridges and humps between the swamps. He saw the trees, the brush, the thickets of fern. He knew exactly which way the land-sloped, how trees protected each place from wind and sun. He saw the winding, narrow driveways, how they'd connect, where fences and gates would have to be placed to keep the big critters away from buildings and the kitchen gardens. And he saw people doing things that were the heartbeats of his own life: cutting firewood, sawing a board, building with stone, bringing the cows in from the back pasture, making hay. And he considered how that little flat — there and there, and there — that he had never gotten to, could be brushed and seeded to pasture, or maybe planted to pine — or, what the hell, hard maple...

He looked at me looking at him, and we just watched each other. Then he took his eyes back to his own landscape. He seemed to be up in the air like an eagle or a turkey buzzard. There was a little car headed out the crooked, long driveway from the back pasture. Hummm, he thought, a screen of white spruce on the windward side would make a dandy snowfence. He realized those folks were going to work. One for sure was a nurse.

It must be fall, he thought, for I can see all four cottages in the back pasture. There's a thin-wisp of blue-grey smoke drifting from each chimney. Hard to tell if that little field of clover is tall enough for a third cutting — if the deer haven't got it all chomped down.

He glanced at me again. There was a flash of aggravation and embarrassment in his look. My face said: I got all day, if you haven't got the gumption to really get inside this possibility, it's no skin off my nose. (Instantly I regretted my snottiness, for his loss would very much be my own. More than I could possibly say.) When I looked back at him, he was hard at it. Only now he had moved to the twenty-acre woods on the east half of the east pasture. He was examining each of my building sites with a grim determination to find fault. The one that aggravated him most was an odd glacial ridge on an almost exact north-south line. It was covered with red pine and a smattering of popple, birch, cherry, maple, and hazel brush. It sat at the back of the forty and peered over the long, skinny alder swamp that was actually the remains of an ancient riverbed. From the crest of that ridge there was a lofty view, to the west, of most of the farm. He saw a log house on top of that ridge, tucked in among pines. Many windows faced west, looking out across the alder swamp to the farm.

His aggravation puzzled me. I watched his face with an even greater attentiveness. Something began to disturb his features, like the shadow of a cloud over an oats field, the way small critters evaporate when a hawk's in the neighborhood. There was — I began to feel an alarming astonishment — there was a look of sorrowful joy on his grizzled face, as if he were seeing a beloved ancestor from beyond the grave. His eyes blurred. Tears began to stream down his cheeks. I saw, suddenly, what he was seeing.

There was an old man in that log house, looking out across the swamp to the fields and farm buildings. He was an old, old man with huge hands, the backs of which were covered with liver spots. He was sitting in a recliner chair by a bay window — obviously his chair and his window — and he was contemplating for the ten thousandth time the pastoral landscape those huge hands had wrought. His hair was snowy white, and his posture was fierce and frail.

He looked at me with such wounded openness that I was immobilized and transfixed. Who are you to dangle the Kingdom of God before me like this? His gaze was relentless. Who are you to advertise such a vision of wholesome living and spiritual discipline? Just who the hell do you think you are?

There was no evasion possible. A goddam hippie pothead I blubbered, my face blubbered. I was stricken. I was in over my head. I was a weakling and a coward.

His gaze impaled me. Don't you know that those who cleared this land have more blood in their veins than you weakwilled pisspots who live in your dopey heads? You who suck on reefers and think community comes through the bulges in your underwear?

It was not, strictly speaking, an accusation. It was oddly also a confession and a plea, as if he were stating a fact he wished wasn't true, as if he were confessing his own sins in the only gruff way he was able, as if he were pleading with me to contradict and overpower him with a greater truth. Tell me the sermon on the mount is true. Better yet, dammit, clean up your life and show me that the commons can be resurrected.

There was no way out of this one. His face was so open. His hurt was so incredibly deep.

I just stood there, feeling totally powerless, and bawled.

Paul Gilk, author of Nature's Unruly Mob *is a woods worker, musician, and former town board member in Lincoln County.*

The Dells

WILLIAM STEUBER

We were in a roar where we were. Such speed as we were making there'd have been roar to a top buggy on a dusty road. Up ahead the roar had a whine to it. A whine like a pipe organ with all the stops out and all the keys held down, like the sound on a platform when an express goes by, like a saw relishing a log, like the pigeons roared when the net sprung. The gorge narrowed so fast the rocks themselves sprang at us like a net, too. The sight and sound took my stomach and all its connections and knotted them around my neck and pulled them tight. If it wasn't for those five drivers manning their sweeps so brave no matter what happened, I'd have laid right down like another bundle of lath and given up.

We hit the rock at the elbow head-on. The forward sweep blade splintered. The sweep pole lifted off its pivot, knocked its three drivers pitching. The one who'd jumped on from the boat sprawled and staggered all the way back where I was before he got his balance. The whole front section sprung boards loose, but didn't break clear. The raft spun around the hung part. Our end cracked into the opposite wall. That snapped the back sweep. Boards on our end buckled and splintered. Right there in front of me I couldn't hear those boards crack loose in all that roar.

The raft stopped and tilted upward, wedged tight between the walls. The water couldn't stop. We weren't a raft any more, but a dam. A wall of water knocked us down and would have swept us off if it wasn't for stakes we grabbed that pinned the boards together and stuck up a foot. The loosened boards went. The broken sweep poles went. All the lath roared off. Bundles of it raked me. The water pulled me straight out like a flag whipping from its staff. If I'd have breathed, I'd have drowned. All I could think, over and over, was, we didn't make it, we didn't make it.

The water set me down again easy on the raft. I opened my eyes. My head was out. I could breathe. The water pressure had broken the raft in two where the cribs joined. We were moving again. We were all alive. Four of us hanging to my two-thirds, two on the other third bumping us. No little shanty, no more sweeps, our two rafts now were swept bare. We were racing again and turning end for end, bumping the sandstone knobs on one side then the other. I recognized those knobs. Mr. Wilcox's Navy Yard.

Stone ships standing still in all that roaring force. Swallows played over us. I never wished for wings so hard. Not the angel wings I'd be judged for any minute, but real wings to get me out of there.

The river widened out again. The whine left the roar and then the roar quieted down. We still slid along pretty fast and without sweeps we'd bump and turn around and around as we went along. Our two rafts traveled the same speed within talking distance of each other. Those drivers could stand now without anything to hang onto. Only when we bumped rocks did we have to hold onto those stakes. "Bet that's the highest water anybody's ever run the Devil's Elbow," came booming across from the other raft.

"Whadda ya mean run it?" one of our drivers hollered back. "We had about as much control as a calf with the shits."

William Steuber is author of The Landlooker, *a Wisconsin classic containing the above excerpt.*

The River

MALCOLM ROSHOLT

It seems beside the point to say that the Chippewa Valley once contained billions of board feet of pine timber. It seems more to the point to say that the Chippewa Valley once held the greatest number of white pine in any area of equal size in the United States.

In most forestland of Wisconsin, there were "openings land," where there were openings in the forest created either by nature or by forest fires. And there were forties covered mostly with brush and occasionally a twisted oak, or willow leaning over the banks of a stream glutted with old windfalls and brush. But in the Chippewa Valley the forest took up five-sixths of the total land area, interspersed by rivers, lakes, swamps, and the Blue Hills.

It was to this heavily forested region that the first lumberman came to live in the 1820s and 1830s to cut down trees, buck them up, skid them to a river and float them down to a sawmill and saw them into square timbers, planks, boards, studdings, shingles, laths and pickets.

Since the timber in the woods could be purchased cheaply, or, as in many cases, stolen from the public domain, it is often thought that most lumbermen became wealthy. Look at the beautiful homes they built in Neillsville, Chippewa Falls, and in Eau Claire. On the contrary, the history of the industry in Wisconsin reveals that lumbering was a risky business in which more men failed than succeeded either as sawmill operators, or as loggers. There seemed to be no end to the natural disasters that lumbermen could fall heir to either by fire in the timber, fire in the mill, or floods, or open winters with not enough snow for good sleighing. Scarcely a year passed without some log boom breaking open sending thousands of logs downstream in a mad stampede. Many drifted ashore and had to be rolled back into the river with horses or oxen. There was a constant struggle to avoid log jams because they cost mill owner delay and added expense.

Any trade, however, attracts entrepreneurs, men of little experience but lots of courage. Yet, without proper management techniques and knowledge of the market for the products they manufactured, these plungers often lost their investment at the slightest setback.

Among the interesting expressions they brought with them was "good chance" and "bad chance." A "good chance" was a tract of timber which might prove profitable; a "bad chance" was one where the risk factor was out of proportion to possible gains. These two expressions seem to epitomize the ups and downs of the lumber industry in the 19th Century.

The hand of man and the whims of nature have changed the Chippewa River in the past century, yet, whatever the changes, it continues to form the watershed for nearly one-sixth of the state of Wisconsin.

The river below the city of Chippewa Falls slows down and can easily be used for lumber rafting, or floating logs. The exciting part of the river once lay between the Falls and mouth of the Flambeau, sixty-eight kilometers (42 miles) or so as the current flowed, and this was referred to in the lexicon of the old river drivers as the "wild Chippewa," for here the river tumbled and pitched down a slope which fell more than seventy meters, through falls once named Little, Brunet, Jim's and through rapids named Paint Creek and Eagle. But all this has changed and that is why it is described in the past tense. The river is almost one long lake today, created by a series of dams extending all the way north of Chippewa Falls to the mouth of the Flambeau.

The most common sources of log jams on the main stem of the Flambeau, that is, below the forks, were at Cedar Rapids, and at Big Falls, north of Ladysmith. Here the river pitched at least twelve meters in three successive rapids. Other rapids on the main stem of the Flambeau were known as "Shaw's Rapids," after Daniel Shaw, "Vinette Rapids," after Bruno Vinette, an early trader and lumberjack, and "Josie Island Rapids," probably named for Malcolm Josie and after whom Josie Creek on the Flambeau is also named. None of these names appear on modern maps of the Flambeau River State Forest.

Malcolm Rosholt lives in Rosholt, Wisconsin and is the author of numerous books on Wisconsin history. He served with the Flying Tigers in China during World War II.

Use the Land Fairly

BILL BERRY

Back in the '70s, I met a gentle, old fellow who lived with his wife in a rustic farmhouse on a bluff overlooking the St. Croix River in western Wisconsin. He had invented an oxygen tablet that could be dropped into a bait bucket, giving extra minutes of life to the little fatheads and shiners meant for anglers' hooks.

The old fellow marketed this tablet across the nation, and it provided him and his wife with a decent living. More than oxygen tablets, I was interested in their old farmhouse and its muted perch, nestled among hardwood trees and an understory of shrubs, grapevines and other plantings they tended there above the St. Croix.

One day I told him how much I admired their little place. Yes, it was a nice home, he allowed, but then he said something else. They had lived there for a long time, he said, and the longer they did, the more he had come to believe that people shouldn't put homes on those bluffs. We just shouldn't live in some places, he said. What I wondered was, why didn't they move? I wondered, but I never mustered the guts to ask him.

Now and then over the years, I've been reminded of that man's words as people chew on that tough nut, the issue of land use. My old boss, George Rogers, a longtime editor of the Stevens Point Journal, often lobbied in his editorials for sensible land use policies. He continued that theme in an environmental and outdoors column he wrote after retiring from the daily grind. When George quit writing that column in 1997, he took note in his goodbye piece of his efforts to keep the issue in the news, and he wryly added that apparently no one had paid any attention, leastwise anyone who was willing or able to do anything about it.

George would sometimes say that many of the strongest opponents of urban sprawl began to champion the issue a few days after paint had dried on their new homes in the country. Another fellow talked along the same lines not too long ago, but not in Wisconsin. He's a friend who had moved from Wisconsin to Colorado a half-dozen years ago. We were touring the Rockies just west of Loveland, Colorado, the city he and his wife had chosen to call home.

The human population in parts of Colorado is growing by leaps and bounds, and the issue of where it's appropriate to put homes is the subject of ongoing and seemingly answerless debate in the shadow of the Rockies. On a drive one day, this friend pointed to the sprawling "show homes," as he called them, the ones springing up on features like the Hogback Range west of Loveland. The Hogback is a long, bald stretch of foothills that we'd call major mountains back home. Out there, it's just the Hogback, a visual prelude to the glorious Rockies. A lot of it is in private hands, and people have taken to building those pricey homes on the Hogback. There they can look down on Loveland to the east and up to the Rockies on the west. An impressive perch, no doubt.

But what about the rest of us? My friend agreed when I decided that those show homes looked like shacks as we tried to look past them to the rugged Rockies. "It's greed and selfishness, is what I figure." That's what my friend said.

My mind flashed back to the gentle fellow who lived and died along the St. Croix. He never seemed greedy or selfish, and his little place was hidden on the bluff, not sticking out like a wart on an index finger. Still, he lived there, where he believed he probably shouldn't.

I think my good friend in Colorado is at least partially wrong. It's not all greed and selfishness. Not everyone who buys a few acres in the country does so to show off. Many are just living out their dreams. They build modest homes and live quietly, closer to the land. Maybe they even improve their little spreads, being more conscious of the land and its needs than some of its earlier occupants.

Some of this migration to the country is a consequence of the back-to-nature urges that grew amidst the social upheavals of the 1960s and '70s. On my shelf is a book called "Living on a Few Acres," a 1978 publication of the U.S. Department of Agriculture. It's a healthy-sized book that coaches people on truck farming, bee keeping, cattle raising and flower growing. It's prelude reads: "Many suburbanites and city people have moved to the country. Those who haven't done so and are thinking about it should study carefully all they can about what is involved before making the move. This book should help."

The ag department aiding and abetting would-be invaders is enough to make your average third generation farmer cringe. But maybe it shouldn't. There's a lot about traditional farming that needs fixing, too, if we're going to do right by the land. I live in a city just north of central Wisconsin's Golden Sands region. On a windy spring day, the sky turns an eerie brown out south of town. Then we know that the sands are shifting, a condition exacerbated by the sway of big pivot irrigation systems, which need wide, open stretches. Many a windbreak has been cleared on the sands to accommodate those big irrigation rigs.

On one of those recent windy spring days, I lent a hand to my friend Bill Horvath, who had 160 trees that needed planting on his land in the Shawano County town of Navarino. This is Horvath's childhood farm. It used to be a mix of woodland and swamp, but it was drained and cropped. It's his idea that the land ought to be returned to what it was, and he's taking advantage of a variety of government programs to do so. In the autumn, we'll hunt waterfowl on the wetlands he has restored. He'll be out there with other friends in November, hunting deer. He doesn't live there, he just goes there, and long after he's died, the land will bear his mark.

Horvath has spent a lifetime in the conservation field, doing long hours for what he calls "God's work." A man who doesn't spare words, it's his belief that land use is the most important environmental issue in America.

His solution? Quit making more humans than the land can handle. Sprawl, he says, is a component of population growth. He was preaching vasectomy to his neighbors 20 years ago. Then you need county boards and town boards that just say no. No to unwise, unreasonable development. No to a home in a woodlot. No to subdivisions on rural lands, even if the subdivider is a third generation farmer who wants to split up a 40 so his kids can each have a chunk.

The reality, unfortunately, is that County Board visionaries who take stands like that quickly become former County Board visionaries. As my friend in Colorado notes, there's money in them there hills, a little bit for a lot of different people every time a home goes up on a mountain perch. It's a process of education, says my friend Bill Horvath, and incremental gains are the best we can achieve.

My two cents? What right does a city dweller have addressing rural land use? As much or more than the country dweller, I maintain. So here you have it.

We as a society need to spend money to repair decaying urban neighborhoods. There's gentle beauty up and down many a city block. Many of our neighborhoods have just gone untended for too long. We need to fix that. We need to fortify low-interest loan programs that help homeowners and landlords revitalize their homes.

And then we need to talk tax equity. We need to make people pay the real costs of living in the country and working in the city. Those who commute to high-tax municipalities for their jobs should help pay the costs of maintaining the infrastructures and services that those communities provide. Right now, the system often punishes urban dwellers with a stiff right cross and a haymaker left hook. They get socked with high property tax bills from the local authorities. Then their county taxes often pay a high percentage of the bill to provide services to rural dwellers, many of whom spend much of their lives at city jobs, on city streets, in city parks.

Maybe a little tax equity and reinvestment in cities, small and large, would preserve some of the rural landscape that we need and cherish. At the very least, it would be fairer to the people who live in population centers and at less cost to the environment.

Bill Berry was editor of the Stevens Point Journal *for 23 years. He now works for CAP Services.*

Wisconsin Landscapes

PHILIP H. LEWIS

To live in a place not so far removed from the time of settlement, with forest places that have never been cut, where a river through wild rice looks like the world had not been touched since time began, where eagles and bears can be seen, and still live in a city is fortunate indeed. Those who live here know fishing, hunting, cultivating and harvesting.

Our natural world is perceived in a variety of ways, ranging from industrial and commercial to the spiritual shrine of untouchable value. With every interpretation between. This is our sense of place. It is the human home — our ecological niche. It is our family. God's creation, the 'ecology' is the balance of power in which we are suspended. Possess still the tantalizing capacity of the primordial to bring forth life.

We are the stewards of all the wonders that surround us. My life's work has been that of a landscape architect devoted to regional design, and the process of guiding development to have the least detrimental impact on our natural and cultural resources in the most economical and pleasing way. I undertook in late 1961 an inventory of the landscape of Wisconsin in the resource planning division of Wisconsin Recreation and Open Space Plan. In 1960 Governor Gaylord Nelson proposed the one-cent sales tax to finance this effort by the Department of Resource Development under David Carley with the aid of such leaders as Harold Jordahl, Jake Beuscher, and Dick Andrews.

Nelson found a sympathetic chord when he reminded the legislators of the "favorite picnic spot that is now a housing development, a wonderful duck marsh that has been drained for farming, a scenic highway stretch that is now cluttered with billboards and roadside stands, a once-secret trout stream that has been encircled and closed off by private land-owners or overrun and heavily pressured by powerboats."

The inventory was to acquire and protect critical natural and cultural resources of the state — those that support tourism and recreation. The process had a profound effect on how land is chosen for purchase by the state. We mapped topography, water and wetlands, vegetation, animal denizens, cultural and historical sites and areas, ethnic settlement patterns, and tourism facilities and related them to transportation, population, climate, land ownership, and land use. The essence was that the greatest resources natural and cultural, lie in environmental corridors. With this goes the knowledge that great chunks of prairie, desert and woodland are desirable for their intrinsic value. When these domains contain the corridor assets they become prime candidates for protection.

All of our land uses modify the environment. The more we tend to determine the impact of development and construct rules governing land use, the more important is consciously determined regional design framework. All our constructed facilities serve the most people in the best way, with the least deleterious effect on the resource base — and at the same time, the achievement of a flexible infra-structure, aesthetically pleasing, integrating material, form and function; with long-term usefulness, that is a daunting goal. Can we settle for less? Of course we do, all the time — this little housing development here and that little shopping center there and a little less wetland and shoreline or more dreary apartment or office blocks — all for the lack of some inspired design, some technical vision of the best possible future. Or maybe just a little questioning of WHAT DOES IT LOOK LIKE? HOW DOES IT WORK? WHAT'S THE BEST WAY TO DO IT?

Design skills are necessary to save access to the lakes and rivers, the forests and fields, hills and prairies, eagles, bears, wolves, birds, fish, wildflowers, frogs, and fireflies. And to save for ourselves the requirements of life itself; clean air, water, food, habitation, clothing, and livelihoods.

Do we have the political will to see how to keep our people, and to keep the places we treasure? We are fortunate in the place we live and the resources at our disposal, but are those resources unlimited? There isn't any more land. Life on another planet is a distant dream and our climate seems to be changing.

Educational efforts are part of the answer. Public participation in planning processes must be more than public hearings on final products. The pieces of the land-use puzzle need to be examined and presented to the public. A range of land use schemes from which to choose is more informative than a single plan. Environmental centers that present resource information in the form of models, displays, and opportunities to observe and take part in the natural world can also be centers that present planning design and land-use information. Such centers, web-sites, and activities are beginning and are finding public acceptance.

The last resort is government. It is clumsy, unreliable, and slow to change. It is also the best thing available to us. Thomas Jefferson's exhortation to inform the public implies that the public will act upon what they know. Not taking part in decisions implies a lack of faith in their effectiveness. Politicians plan their public selves to conform to the polling process, but the polling seems to omit those factors most vital to our existence (clean air, water, land, products, etc.). We must take our government to account for environmental and planning design decisions starting with neighborhoods and reaching out to intergovernmental relations and the global economy. This is not an original idea, it seems to appear in every publication and public informational medium. Remember clear sunny days, clean rain, good food to eat and urban places of classic beauty when election day comes.

Phil Lewis is perhaps best known as the person responsible for the innovative work in urban design that brought national attention to the concept of sprawl.

Of Frogs and Us

WILL FANTLE

In my younger years, I recall gunning my motorcycle around the winding roads of rural Eau Claire County. One spring evening a rinsing shower freshened the land, marking the trail ahead of me with a twisting, twirling mist. Astride my crotch rocket, I sped down the country lane.

My path grew suddenly thick with migrating frogs, and green-slicked in my wake. There was no avoiding it; my scoot knifed into their spring odyssey, the churning tires smashing a green, pink and crimson montage into the asphalt. I felt some mild pangs of regret over my unintended bloody grindings, but in my ignorance I figured I was a manly man and it's the way of the world.

Since that time, an entire generation of kids and their parents have absorbed a different perspective on frogs. Television — that tube with a view — brought us the antics and insights of Kermit the Frog. I think Kermit helped humanize these green skinned beasts. This magical Muppet built a cross-generational bond of identification with and affection towards frogs. And I think it's a big reason why so many in our society harbor such deep anxiety and alarm towards what's appearing on and near the lily pads of our waters.

You've probably heard about it — the bizarre, misshapen frogs with three, five and even six legs, missing eyes and eye sockets, and warped sexual organs. Their plight speaks hauntingly — near the end of the millennium, is this a message from our backyards?

As I write this, I'm staring at a photo I snapped of a six-legged leopard frog found in northwestern Wisconsin. I recently saw the creature at the Milwaukee Public Museum where Midwestern scientists and researchers had gathered to discuss the strange frog happenings. Hearing of a live sample, I knew I had to see it and I managed to talk my way up to the off-limits 6th floor of the museum for a secluded showing.

My guide popped the lid from the frog's temporary Tupperware home and lifted it onto the lab table. I was the circus voyeur. The source of the frog's freakiness was its right rear hip where three legs jutted from the junction with its body. One of the three looked relatively normal, two were grossly deformed spindles splayed at weird angles.

I never saw the frog leap. I suspect its jumps would wobble along crooked lines making it a tempting target for a swift predator. Instead, the frog sat calmly and tolerated my camera pushing into its space for close-up shots. I privately thanked the frog for allowing my intrusion into its personal nightmare.

Now before you jump down my throat for such fuzzy, muddy feelings (sheesh, he's thanking a geeky frog for a freaking photograph ....), let me explain that if I thought my own survival hinged on gobbling the critter, I wouldn't hesitate — though I'd probably cook and saute it first. But I don't think that's the case.

No longer a tadpole, I believe in and respect the right of frogs and all of the earth's other lifeforms to share existence with me on this planet. Their health and their vitality mirrors my own condition, our own condition. I learn by peering into this reflection.

Downstairs, the 250 scientists attentively followed the tightly packed summaries of field research and investigative findings presented by their colleagues. Wisconsin, it turns out, has recorded the third highest total of amphibian deformities in the country, following only Minnesota and Vermont. I mention amphibians because toads and salamanders are experiencing similar distortions. Upstairs, a five-legged salamander, found near Stoughton, rested in its solitary Tupperware home.

Amphibians possess an extremely permeable skin — what's in the water, air, and soil easily enters their bodies. The researchers at this gathering are using this quality to explore several theories — test frogs are exposed to various combinations of pesticides, ultra-violet radiation (like what causes sunburns), and probed for parasites to determine the source of the problem.

I know the value of such testing, it will help pinpoint what's at work here. But I also can't help but feel a little troubled by the poisoning, maiming, and dissecting done in the name of figuring out what's poisoning and maiming amphibians. Many of the scientists at this meeting probably entered amphibian studies (herpetology) because they relished stomping around marshes, wetlands, and swamps as kids. As students, though, they learned to submerge that delight while hacking, slicing, flaying, and inspecting the inner workings and guts of frogs and other critters.

To me this devaluing of the lives of "lesser" species indicates how detached and removed we are from the planetary pulse of life. And to the bull-headed believer in the superiority of "man," I submit that if we're so smart, how come frogs have the good sense to slumber through our long, dark, cold Wisconsin winters?

One measure of our nature seems our ability to hold competing, contradictory ideas while slogging forward through life. I like science and what it reveals of us and the world we dwell in; yet I ponder the price.

All right, so what are the scientists saying? The emerging evidence blames pesticides. The poisons mess with developmental codes early in life, then warp adult amphibian bodies. I wonder how wise it is for us to drink, swim and recreate in the same locales mutating these creatures.

In Minnesota, a common insecticide sprayed across the Land of 10,000 Lakes in their endless war on mosquitoes seems a culprit. One Minnesota researcher has handled as many as 200 deformed frogs during an afternoon of field investigations.

It also doesn't appear that we're finding more strangely shaped frogs simply because we're looking for them. Decades of recorded outdoor observations, which permit a comparison between today and yesterday, shouts no to this possibility. In fact, scientists returning to the original locations of field work done in the 1950's and '60's are uncovering even more disturbing news — a dramatic decline in certain species of frog populations. It's not as graphically newsy as the image of six-legged frogs, but it's more serious.

"It's not easy being green," Kermit the Frog told his many listeners. If you spend any time this year among Wisconsin's bountiful waters, take a moment, cup your ear, listen. Can you hear a message?

Will Fantle is an activist/writer from Eau Claire who contributes features and news reports to Wisconsin-based weeklies and magazines.

Rights in the Land

H. C. JORDAHL, JR.

Thirty years ago, my wife and I purchased an abandoned dairy farm in rural Richland County. With my children we began the task of healing the land. The results are now evident. Our modest efforts, along with nature's incredible capacity to heal, provide us with a pleasurable view of forested hills, woodland openings and a hay field cupped in a valley floor.

I plan to place perpetual restrictions on the use of the land — a conservation easement — which will preclude subdivision and require stewardship on the part of future owners. Though simple in concept, the translation to legal language which will stand is difficult. For guidance, I turned to the past to glimpse insights into an uncertain future. One fact became crystal clear: change is inevitable.

So often in our arrogance, we date land use history with the advent of the first pioneers. A somewhat longer view took me back to the Paleo Indians who were here some 10,000 years before white settlers. Indeed, the bones of a mastodon killed by a spear used by these nomadic people were found a few miles from the farm. Much later, the Sauk, Ho Chunk (Winnebago) and the Fox Indians treaded lightly on the land, leaving only artifacts, which we find and treasure today.

The ancient peneplain was eroded by wind and water leaving deep river valleys and high rocky ridges and cliffs. Glacial meltwater found a crevice in a sandstone cliff nearby and eroded a tunnel leaving a natural bridge through which the West Branch of the Pine River flows.

The river valleys — the Kickapoo, Pine and Wisconsin Rivers — provided barriers to fires which periodically swept much of southern Wisconsin leaving oak savanna landscapes. My farm developed into a mesic forest dominated by shade tolerant trees — hard maple, elm, white pine, basswood, cherry. Arid ridges and rock escarpments supported oak, hickory and prairie remnants.

A public road traversed my farm and adjacent lands. The road, two miles in length, served not only my land but four other dairy farms. Today, the dairy farms are gone, now marked only by residences, my house and a silo foundation 100 yards from the first settler's cabin.

Dairying lasted about 100 years before the soil was impoverished. The owners of my land abandoned the farm and moved to town. To buy the property, I bid against five other parties, and paid double the expected price. Today, my urban friends view my price as obscenely low, farmer neighbors think it obscenely high. In my first encounter with a neighbor, irate over a missing heifer, "I don't know why the hell you bought this God-forsaken place and your fences need fixing." A second farmer wondered what I had paid for such a messed up place. He likewise told me to fix my fences.

I was discouraged after an initial walk through the farm. The roads were gullied, gashes on the valley slopes were 15 or more feet deep, over-grazed hillsides were barren. The settlers lacking knowledge and experience, did their best to survive here for a century. But the land and mismanagement beat them.

Eight to twelve inches or more of the tillable land eroded and has lost its original fertility. Hillside and hilltop grazing and uncontrolled or purposely set fires cleared out the brush and greened up the pasture but devastated the forest.

We fenced to control livestock from neighboring farms. Gullies were filled with dirt, farm roads were fertilized and seeded, and new trails and water diversions constructed. Thousands of white pine and black walnut trees and wildlife shrubs were planted. Farm debris—rusting threshing rigs, hay mowers, junked cars and other evidences of an earlier civilization — were removed. Small ponds were constructed for recreation, erosion and flood control.

To remedy the abuse of the past, a remedial timber harvest was conducted. Undesirable trees and shrubs—ironwood, prickly ash, sumac, hickory-were cut to open up the forest canopy and to encourage the regeneration of oak, pine, maple, basswood, cherry.

In the absence of grazing and fire which favored oak, I maintain a few openings for that species for their beauty, value for lumber, and abundant acorn crops, a wildlife food. In the long run, acid precipitation and global warming will change the tree species making up the forest. Drought through natural weather cycles or exacerbated by inefficient burning of fossil fuels, could have a dramatic impact on forest survival.

So when I draft my easement I can be certain of only a few things. As long as our democracy survives, division of most of the farm into residential use will be precluded. In sharp contrast to what is occurring in much of rural Wisconsin; the division of land suitable for recreation and aesthetics into smaller and smaller parcels, each with a seasonal cabin or permanent home.

The new residents put primary emphasis on quietness, scenic beauty and watching wildlife, not on land management. As the wild lands around homes are domesticated, there will be changes in wildlife numbers and species. Hunting may well be precluded. My land will become an island and perhaps an oasis for plants and animals requiring larger areas.

The organization to whom I dedicate my subdivision rights — a private land trust — wants assurance that I and subsequent owners will practice stewardship. Thus, a forest management plan is required. This I can plan for the short run, say 50 years, or perhaps for a century but after that change is certain.

Short-term costs — capital investment, taxes, management and maintenance — will be partially offset by income from hay and timber. Reduced property taxes will result from subdivision constraints. In the long term, the value of the tract of land will increase. Any net dollar loss will be compensated for by my family's and friends' enjoyment of the land.

As I enumerate these values, I'm mindful our society is responsible for both creating and protecting them.

When I give away "the rights" to my land, it is in the hope subsequent owners will be guided by my language and the knowledge that change in the land is inevitable. Hopefully, the future owners will understand and work with that change, and be guided by an intuitive and ethical sense. Permitting the land to respond positively and naturally.

H. C. "Bud" Jordahl, Jr., is Professor Emeritus, Department of Urban and Regional Planning, UW-Madison and University Extension.

Restoring Roots to a Region's Wetlands

PATRICK DURKIN

Maybe it's experience with root erosion that explains my soft-spot for the lost river cane, wild celery and weed-beds that once cloaked lakes Poygan, Winneconne and Butte des Morts in east-central Wisconsin.

When flying over the expansive lakes or viewing them in aerial photographs, you struggle to believe they weren't always open water. But then someone digs out duck hunting photographs taken nearly 100 years ago, and there's the proof. Locals who know their turf look past the hunters and their rows of hanging ducks, and point out landmarks to convince skeptics.

Which reminds me of my experience with root erosion. Much as the big lakes lost much vegetation to uprooting, I've lost almost all the hair atop my head. And much like photographic evidence of the lakes' past, I must use identifiable features to convince people that the guy in some 1980s photo is me.

"See, there's the big schnoz, cleft chin, and bar-door gap between the front chompers!"

"Whoa. That is you, isn't it? Giggle."

Unlike the lakes, my hair's uprooting was painless and caused no lasting damage. And unlike my hair, the lakes stand a chance of regrowing. In the lakes' case, however, it's taking vision and effort, not vanity and Rogaine.

We can now watch volunteer conservationists and the Department of Natural Resources build rock break-walls around once lush wetlands. And we can read and listen as they plan to restore nesting islands and marsh plants within the walls. But all the while, we know these are merely first steps in rejuvenating the wetland habitat. Most of us won't see the project in full bloom until long after the blush has left our own flower. If then.

To understand the restoration efforts on lakes Poygan, Winneconne and Butte des Morts, we must remember its roots in the 1960s when hunters, trappers and other conservationists watched huge chunks of marshlands floating toward Oshkosh in spring. Not until the mid-1980s, however, did people start uniting behind DNR biologists like Ron Bruch and Art Techlow to stop it.

Before Bruch and Techlow began marshaling the public's force, they asked everyone to recall the region's geologic and economic history. Not until everyone understood the forces that washed away the wetlands could they try to restore them.

Until the lower Fox River was dammed about 120 years ago to raise water levels for commercial boats and barges, the lakes were 3 to 5 feet lower than today. As the waters were continually held at artificially high levels, wild rice, river cane and underwater weeds drowned out.

This process exposed fertile bottoms to waves, which continually churned up dirt and suspended it in the water. In turn, the turbid water blocked sunlight from reaching the bottom, which prevents regrowth. As more open water took over, wind-whipped waves washed away even more weeds, exposing even more bottom to churning and suspension.

Lake weeds, both underwater and above, need calm, clear, relatively shallow waters to take root. Because it's unrealistic and economically unfeasible to remove dams on the lower Fox, the only solution was to build the break-walls now under construction. These walls will provide the plants and soil sanctuary from relentless wave action, allowing protected areas to recapture their past habitat.

Perhaps many years from now, those photos of 1890s duck hunters on Butte des Morts won't look so foreign to us.

Patrick Durkin is editor of Deer and Deer Hunting *magazine. He writes conservation and outdoors columns for several Wisconsin newspapers.*

An Ecological Play on a Stage Known as Dunlap Hollow

STANLEY A. TEMPLE

Wisconsin's landscapes rarely remain stable for long; they are dynamic and shift with environmental fluctuations. Like the stage of a long-running play with many acts, a landscape changes and characters move on and off stage. The pace of the action on a landscape stage may be imperceptibly slow or terribly swift, but it is inevitable that the scenery and the actors will change, regardless of how attached some members of the audience may have become to the previous act.

As members of the audience, individual human beings do not live long enough to witness many of the long-term twists and turns in the plot of the ecology play taking place on their favorite landscape. Most will see and appreciate only the few acts during their brief lifetime. Only with a playbill can they know what has happened in previous acts and what lies ahead. For ecological plays on the stage of a natural landscape, the most insightful descriptions of past and future acts are usually written by ecologists who understand the plot and know how the sets and characters change.

As an ecologist, I have analyzed the plot of the play unfolding on the landscape stage in which I now live: the seven-square-mile watershed in northwestern Dane County called Dunlap Hollow. I will share the plot with you because it provides a microcosm of other ecological plays unfolding on landscapes throughout Wisconsin.

The curtain rises on the Dunlap Hollow stage some 12,000 years ago, near the end of the Pleistocene glaciation. The edge of a massive sheet of ice is located just at the head of the hollow. The flora and fauna are species adapted to cold, wet conditions of arctic tundra. The first play is the "Milankovitch cycle," a complex series of oscillations that change the world's climate in predictable ways with the shift of the earth's orbit. This cycle brought the glaciers to the hollow as the climate cooled, and then melted them as the climate inevitably warmed.

But, the plot of the play was predictable, and the subsequent changes brought the inevitable. As the climate warmed, plants and animals returned to the stage in an orderly progression. The first cast to take center stage were boreal forest plants and animals — spruce and moose and other coniferous forest species. Their act was relatively short, and in subsequent acts, some were eliminated by a new arrival, Homo sapiens. Most, however, were displaced by the northward-migrating deciduous forest and its characteristic biota.

As the Milankovitch cycle progressed, the climate became steadily warmer and drier, allowing a new cast of characters to enter from the south and west. For a time Dunlap Hollow may have looked like a Wisconsin "desert," as a hot, dry climate and sandy, well-drained soils gave a decidedly arid character. Some of the cast members of this xeric act remain on stage, finding refuge on the hollow's south-facing, sandy slopes where hot, dry conditions still persist. Predictably, the climate again began to turn, and increasingly cooler, moister conditions have prevailed ever since.

With the arrival of European immigrants in the mid-1800s the pace of change quickened and actors began to replace one another more rapidly. We have a good record of what the stage was like when the new actors took over. Descriptions of the original land surveys reveal a picture of Dunlap Hollow in the 1840s.

The survey notes for my property, which lies in the very middle of the hollow, are revealing. Moving north along the Township line, the surveyors found only scattered oak trees in a prairie landscape. As they approached the bottom of the valley, they noted that they were in a wet, "low prairie" and that the surrounding hillsides were covered with prairie, scattered oaks and cedars, and clumps of low-quality oak. Though they were within a few feet of Dunlap Creek, they made no mention of running water, only a few springs that seeped into the wet prairies and ferns on the valley's floor. They rolled stones from the hillside to erect a cairn, since there were no "witness" trees to mark the corner.

Soon after this survey, settlers moved in and the prairies on the lower slopes of the hollow were plowed into agricultural fields; the prairies and savannas on steeper ground were converted to pastures; large timber was cut for building material and fuel, and wild fires were suppressed. With the suppression of fire and changes in grazing practices, the pastures on the hillsides were invaded by trees, and young forest replaced savannas and prairies.

Today, most of the non-crop land in Dunlap Hollow is forested, with only a few, open-grown oaks embedded within the woods as reminders that not too long ago the area was a savanna. Because the valley floor was too wet to farm, it was drained by a ditch that would eventually be called Dunlap Creek, now a conspicuous feature in the hollow.

But the play goes on. The script is now being written by new directors who are the current landowners in the hollow. Many purchased marginal farmland taken out of agricultural production over the past 30 years and no longer work the land. According to a recent survey many of these new owners are interested in making their land more "natural," but have understandable difficulties identifying what natural means in a landscape that has changed as much as Dunlap Hollow.

The reactions of some neighbors to the types of ecological restorations that I am undertaking on my property are illustrative. Thinning an overgrown oak savanna on a prominent hillside by logging younger trees and leaving scattered, older oaks was viewed by some as destroying a forest, not recreating a savanna. The burning of the prairie remnant on my property was generally viewed as a positive-if-hazardous activity, but the burning of my fire-starved wetland that was degrading from a species-rich mosaic of wet prairies and fens to overgrown shrub was viewed more suspiciously. Our efforts to keep purple loosestrife out of the upstream wetlands and the DNR's experiments with biological control were viewed as eccentric discrimination against a pretty plant.

Our efforts on behalf of rare, wildlife species, such as ornate box turtles and eastern bluebirds, were well received, but our desire to retain the timber rattlesnake in the hollow was considered positively daft.

What exactly should owners in Dunlap Hollow do with their land? Their decisions determine the next act in the land play.

My crystal ball is murky, I suspect that many will "let nature take its course," which means they'll not take an active role in directing the future of their land. This passive approach to land management has predictable consequences. If today's oak roasts are not restored to oak savannas or prairies and burned regularly, they will eventually turn into maple-dominated forests. If prairie remnants are not burned and weeded, they will be taken over by woody vegetation and exotic weeds and eventually become forests. If wetlands are not burned and weeded, they will be invaded by more woody plants and exotics, resulting in the loss of species-rich wetland communities.

I would wish for my neighbors to become active managers of the ecological features of their land, to better understand the ecology of the hollow. I would hope that the community of landowners in the hollow could work together to restore parts of the Dunlap hollow to what they were like at the time the land surveyors described the area.

Regardless, the ecological play will continue on the land on the stage of Dunlap Hollow. Whether my brief stint on the stage will have long-term consequences for the plot remains to be seen.

Stanley A. Temple is the Beers-Bascom Professor in Conservation in the UW-Madison's Department of Wildlife Ecology. He is a past Chairman of the Wisconsin Chapter of The Nature Conservancy and a past President of the Society for Conservation Biology.

Milwaukee in the Great Depression

FRANK ZEIDLER

During the 1930's several people in the movement exhibited attitudes and actions which would allow a description of the modern environmentalist. The most colorful of these persons was Walter G. Bubbert, a University of Wisconsin student in landscaping. Walker left numerous slides of parks, gardens, and county fairs. These slides were given to the Milwaukee County Historical Society.

Another of these persons was Max Weber, a German army veteran of four years in the First World War. Weber was a professional gardener. Theodore and Auguste Mueller were associated with the group. They were German immigrants who had lived on Pierron's Isle in the Milwaukee River during the heart of the Depression.

The group were strong supporters of the work of Charles B. Whitnall, who in the 1930s had already achieved a national reputation on landscape and park planning, and after whom a park is named at Hales Corners, Wisconsin. The group also had the benefit of contact with Ernest Untermann, one time Director of the Milwaukee County Zoo. Untermann was a zoologist and also a painter of landscapes and wild life.

Giving counsel to this group was the former Mayor of Milwaukee Emil Seidel, who himself was a painter of natural life scenes. Seidel toward the end of his life lived in Garden Homes, the early planned cooperative housing develop on Milwaukee's North Side.

This group helped give impetus to the administration of Mayor Daniel W. Hoan to acquire the lands of Milwaukee Harbor and Lake Front, and also encouraged the development of the extensive Milwaukee County Park system.

The group had contact with several able land use planners of Milwaukee city and county governments, notably Elmer Krieger, City of Milwaukee planner. This group helped create a public acceptance of land use planning and development that characterized Milwaukee until about 1960.

The impetus for environmental development which this relatively small group of individuals created carried over well into the 1950s when the City of Milwaukee doubled its size, engaged in clearing blight areas and building low cost housing, and expanded playgrounds. City beautification through forestry was also emphasized.

These individuals believed that workers should live in a decent, life-sustaining environment. They believed that when working men left the dusty and noisy shop at the end of the day, they were anxious to recover from this hostile environment by being in a home with a yard or spending a weekend day in a public park. Whitnall at one time said that a man is nourished as much by his environment as he is by his stomach. Our movement was as much concerned about the environmental conditions under which life was lived as by hours, wage, and conditions of work.

Frank Zeidler is former Mayor of Milwaukee and leader of the Socialist Party. The above reflections are drawn from an essay entitled "Socialist Environmentalists in the Great Depression."

The Coffee Cup

GEORGE HESSELBERG

"Guy who owned it died," said my dad.

The Ford dealership was sold.

"Guy who bought it is going to close it," said my mom.

The VFW ice skating rink in the park was closed.

"Hasn't been run in years," said my dad.

So it went Thanksgiving weekend in the village of Bangor, population over 1,000, but no café, no Ford dealer and no skating rink.

Are all villages doomed to be visited by observers of my generation wondering what happened to all the condiments that made growing up small a delicious experience?

Every time I go home I notice another piece missing from my childhood. Sometimes pieces are revealed today that I never really understood when I was growing up.

The cafe, the car dealer and the ice rink were all connected with a winter routine any kid would covet today. The VFW put its letters on the outside of a run-down warming house at the village park. There was organ music if someone was around who could figure out the record player. There were games of crack-the-whip and pum-pum-pull-away and there were chances to skate close to girls. If a kiss was involved, Dutch Creek was right next to the rink and if it was frozen over a kid and his girl could skate a half mile up creek to where a fallen tree provided a comfortable bench.

With thighs burning from cold and skates slung over our shoulders, we would walk past sad-eyed Frank Wegner's Ford dealership and through "downtown," then stop to burn our lips on the rim of a mug of thick hot chocolate at the Coffee Cup Café.

I never thought of the journey as romantic or idyllic or even charming, then or now. It was just easy.

Last weekend I walked the tracks — now a state bicycle path — behind my parents' home to the village park and added to my list of missing landmarks.

What happened to the old Bangor Farmer's Co-Op Creamery brick building, where I once cleaned milk tanks and hooped Cheddar before school with the Wegner boys and the Nicolai boys and Billy Bosshard and

Bob Gehrke? Bob Gehrke died long ago from driving too fast and all that remains of the creamery are a storage area and the garage and a store where someone sells cheese made somewhere else.

Who is living in Frank Stark's house, the bachelor guy who was so surprised one Halloween night by the arrival of my brother and me that he gave us each a dime?

Who bought Vilas Johnson's old house, the shoe repair guy? Didn't the Johnsons have a daughter?

Did Leona Vehrenkamp, the school cook with the braid around her head, die? Joe Thicke, the English teacher who killed himself, rented a room in her house.

While those losses add up slowly for the residents, the holiday visitors get the news all at once. The missing structures and businesses are the most noticeable: the shoe store, the hardware store, the dime store, the drugstore, the bar, the pool hall, two grocery stores, the meat market, the two cafes, the Ford and the Chevy dealers, and, perhaps the sorriest loss, the Milwaukee Road depot. Some have replacements: two hair salons, an upscale gift shop, a notions shop, a bigger bank building, a nice flower shop. And the feed mills are still operating, and the bowling alley, and the barbershop and, naturally, the funeral parlor.

Those visits home for the holidays sometimes end up in "who's dead and who's still here" conversations at the kitchen table.

It's more difficult to catalog the missing people, the people for whom I mowed lawns and shoveled sidewalks, some gone without a trace, which is hard to understand in so small a society.

"What happened to so and so?" I will ask, the very presence of a vacant lot reminding me of who lived there when I whistled past those mysteriously dark windows many years ago.

"Long gone," my dad will say.

Coming back, I drove the back roads out of Bangor, up to county Highway Y, road-hunting past the old abandoned farms on the ridge, over Highway 27 and eventually on to Westby, Viroqua, Readstown (Frank's Liquidators, "We Sell Stuff for Peanuts") and beyond.

The farther I got down the road, the more I rationalized about changes.

I figured if the kids in Bangor in 1994 want to ice skate, they can surely wait until the creek freezes, but I worry about the loss of the Coffee Cup Cafe and the chance to get a cup of hot chocolate with marshmallows in a Wisconsin village on a cold winter night.

George Hesselberg is a columnist for the Wisconsin State Journal *and author of* Paint Me Green: Call Me Fern.

The Lucky Ones Live in Wisconsin

JOHN GURDA

The United States is the land of my birth,
The strongest and wealthiest country on earth.
But the states aren't all equal, I'm sorry to say -
Wisconsin's the pick of the fifty today.

I like Virginia, Montana, and Maine,
But it's here in Wisconsin I proudly remain,
With walleyes and fish fries and hot apple pie,
And the Badgerland motto: Eat Cheese or Die.

> **1st Chorus**
> We've got forests and prairies,
> Breweries and dairies,
> Skiing on water and skiing on snow.
> From Big Bend to Bayfield,
> Potosi to Plainfield,
> The lucky ones live in Wisconsin.

Arizona's too dry, Colorado's too high,
In Alaska you'll freeze and in Georgia you'll fry.
Hawaii's so distant it's barely existent,
California is crumbling; let's all wave goodbye.

Nevada's too empty, the deserts don't tempt me.
In Kansas a forest is one lonesome tree.
New York is an anthill, a flesh-and-blood landfill,
And too many lawyers run loose in D.C.

> **2nd Chorus**
> We've got silos and steeples
> And down-to-earth people,
> Holsteins aplenty and Guernseys galore.

From Lone Rock to Lena,
New Glarus to Neenah,
The lucky ones live in Wisconsin.

Minnesota and Michigan, they're both our special friends.
We get along fine with the people next door.
Illinois, on the other hand, I couldn't recommend.
It's flat as a pancake and spoiled to the core.

The Flatlanders visit us year after year,
Clogging the highways and killing our deer.
They root for the White Sox, they frighten our livestock.
We hide all the children whenever they're here.

3rd Chorus
We've got sweet corn and bratwurst,
Chicago's a lot worse.
Our cheddar is better, our butter's the best.
From Monroe to Milwaukee,
Waupun to Wausaukee,
The lucky ones live in Wisconsin

Yes, from Adell to Algoma,
Two Rivers to Tomah,
The lucky ones live in Wisconsin.

John Gurda is a writer, historian, and seven-time winner of the Wisconsin State Historical Society's Award of Merit.

Spirits

A Eulogy

BEN LOGAN

There has been a death in the family. A faithful friend and companion, age approximately 107, a part of so many lives and so many memories, surrendered to a tornado on July 15th, 1997. The name was Big Maple. It stood in the front yard of the ridgetop farm called Seldom Seen.

Big Maple became known to a larger public in my book, *The Land Remembers.* Hundreds of "pilgrims," who visited or wrote letters over the years, had recognized the tree as a central character in the book. Those who came by wanted to lay their hands on its bark, make physical connection with what had been only words on paper.

Since the tree's end, pilgrims touch the massive stump and try to decipher the undecipheral growth rings. Children instantly run to the stump, climb up on it and stand tall there, like new growth.

Big Maple was planted, with the help of her father, by Josephine Mullaney in 1890. She was six years old and had been born in a one-room log cabin a quarter of a mile to the east. When she was one-year old, her family moved into the then new two-story log house that is still part of my home. Josephine Mullaney told me all this when, at age 85, she first read *The Land Remembers.* "Surely," she said, "there is something left of me on that ridge farm. The tree, and perhaps where the birdfoot violets grew by the old log bridge."

Big Maple died quietly. Watching through the dining room window, I saw it fall, the wind roar so loud the tree seemed to come down without a sound. Relaxed, almost detached, as I had learned to be in war during moments of crisis, I found myself asking, "If a tree falls fifteen feet from me without making a sound, what does that mean?"

Big Maple was a responsible friend to the end. It put down two limbs like elbows which took the force of the fall. Top branches snapped off and blew on over the house. Father, who once started to cut the tree, need not have worried as he did each time a storm swept our ridge. The total damage: a dent in the ridgecap, some cracked wooden shingles and a split facia board. Even the birdfeeder was spared, a limb going carefully on each side of it.

These are the facts of Big Maple's demise, but as with any friend, it is its life that is important.

I was born in 1920. The tree was already called Big Maple when I first remember it, and it was already an extension of the house, a warm-weather living room. There were few summer, late spring or early fall evenings when all of us — Father, Mother, us four boys, and hired man Lyle — were not there under the tree. With fireflies floating close above the lawn and whippoorwills calling, the tree gathered us again into a family after a day that had scattered us to tasks all over the farm. Chores were finished, the cows taken to night pasture. A cooling breeze played in the leaves above us, seeming to ease the fatigue of the day.

Mother, often mending clothes or darning socks under the tree, was a reminder in those days that a woman's work seemed never done. She loved the tree. We all knew that. Partly, it was because the tree was home to orioles and a perching place for singing meadowlarks and those hoarse-voiced harbingers of spring, the rusty black-birds. Most of all, I think, she loved the tree because it gave us a time and place of unity. The rest of us often worked together, with time for talk and even moments of play, but she was alone much of the day. Eventide brought her family back to her.

It was a time for reflection, for thinking thoughts and saying words to each other that often had little to do with work and the farm. The talk was mostly adult talk, a kind of lazy pursuing of ideas, beliefs and stories.

I didn't know this then, but the front lawn under the sheltering Big Maple was surely my first schoolhouse, perhaps the best kind of education there is because I did not know I was being educated. My brothers and I might be running from tree to tree in the game we called Little Joe Otter, but we were also hearing the conversation between Father, Mother and the hired man. The values were clear. The duty to neighbors and community were revealed. The importance of honesty and trust became the central point of some story about a local happening.

Neighbors sometimes joined those conversations, bringing us an odd diversity of lives, ideas and fiercely held opinions. When they left us, we could hear their fading voices, the talk that had come alive under the tree still going on as their flickering kerosene lanterns guided them back to their own homeplace.

Yes, the Big Maple is gone, but we do not lose what is true and important. Under the tree I found my clearest sense of the wholeness of that family I was part of — part of without question, good days or bad. Now, the members of my family, and the Big Maple, too, are continuing characters in my life-story.

Big Maple was preceded in death by its planter, Josephine Mullaney, by Father, Mother, Lyle and my brother Sam Junior. Father had been wrong when he said the tree would destroy the house. (He never trusted it as my mother did.) Lyle was wrong, too. He had said it would outlast us all. I, my brother Lee and brother Laurance survive.

More importantly, the Big Maple survives, in story and memory, an important reminder that humans are not separated from all the other living parts and places and mysteries of what Aldo Leopold called THE LAND - all things on, over and in the earth. When I first heard him say that in a University of Wisconsin classroom, it was a moment of great discovery. His definition of land included me, made a place for me in the immense mosaic of life.

Thus it is that I feel no strangeness in saying there has been a death in the family.

Ben Logan is author of The Land Remembers *and many other works.*

The Ojibway Creation Story

EDWARD BENTON BANAI

It has been many years since the Waterdrum has sounded its voice here. This Waterdrum that I have beside me was handed down from my grandfathers. I am preparing this place to be a place of rebirth for traditional Indian ways. This will be a journey to rediscover a way of life that is centered on the respect for all living things. It will be a journey to find the center of ourselves so that we can know the peace that comes from living in harmony with powers of the Universe.

Take these words that I seek to put down and use them in a good way. Use them to teach your children about the way life has developed for the Native people of this country. Use them to redirect your life to the principles of living in harmony with the natural world.

On the surface of the Earth, all is given Four Sacred Directions — North, South, East, and West. Each of these directions contributes a vital part to the wholeness of the Earth. Each has physical powers as well as spiritual powers, as do all things.

When she was young, the Earth was filled with beauty. All of the parts of life lived in harmony with each other.

There were a few people in each of the tribes that have survived to this day who have kept alive their teachings, language, and religious ceremonies. Although traditions may differ from tribe to tribe, there is a common thread that runs throughout them all. This common thread represents a string of lives that goes back all the way to Original Man.

Today, we need to use this kinship of all Indian people to give us the strength necessary to keep our traditions alive. No one way is better than another. I have heard my grandfathers say that there are many roads to the High Place. We need to support each other by respecting and honoring the "many roads" of all tribes. The teachings of one tribe will shed light on those of another.

Eddie Benton Banai is a teacher of spiritual and cultural traditions. This excerpt is from the Mishomis Book *and is used with the permission of* News *from* Indian Country, *Hayward, Wisconsin.*

Letter from the Old Order to the New World Order

BY THE OLD ORDER AMISH CHURCHES OF WILTON, HILLSBORO, LA VALLE, LOGANSVILLE, READSTOWN, VIROQUA, CHASEBURG AND CASHTON, WISCONSIN.

Dear Lt. Col. Adams,

Over 300 years ago our ancestors in Europe were forced to move from place to place to survive severe persecution. Later they found a permanent home and freedom of religion in Pennsylvania where the first law guaranteed "That no person...who professes him or herself Obliged In Conscience to live peaceably and quietly under civil government, shall in any case be molested or prejudiced for his, or her conscientious persuasion or practice."

Here, our forefathers tilled the soil and handed down from generation to generation the religious values and traditions that preserve our "old way." These include continuing to do all fieldwork with horses without the assistance of motorized vehicles.

However, 29 years ago, increased population and heavy traffic forced a small group of Amish farmers to come to the Kickapoo Valley area of Wisconsin, in search of the peace of a less-populated area. Others followed and our farming communities of about 625 families continue to grow.

We are writing to you because we are shocked and saddened to hear that the Air National Guard plans two new air corridors in which, each year, 2,151 training flights will fly at levels as low as 100 feet — over an area in which approximately 5,000 Amish people live. We plead with you to stop this plan because it would be alien and disastrous to our entire, simple, way of life including our religious beliefs, physical safety, and livelihood.

Our religious beliefs are derived from the Old and New Testaments — The Word of God — and are rooted in a deep reverence for pacifism which would be shattered by the continued presence of military bombers in the skies. Pacifism is at the core of our everyday life and unites us in love for our rural life and in fellowship with one another. Our spiritual life is extremely important to us and to this end we meet throughout the week. We also meet on Sundays when all the communities gather together in different believers' homes to hear the Word of God preached. The Air National Guard's low-flying jets would not only disrupt our peaceful worship with high decibel noise, but also infringe on our Christian religious pacifist beliefs as visual symbols of war rending the heavens overhead us.

Our physical safety would be endangered by low-level flights and all ages of our communities would be at risk. We daily contend with the fact that animals startled by noise often instinctively react in panic to either natural or other sounds — such as those made by motor vehicles. Because we Amish are so often behind horses during our day-to-day rural activities, we cannot stress enough the danger we would be exposed to by the roar of low-flying jets.

Our strict "Old Order" Amish religion prohibits the use of rubber tires and the use of motorized vehicles unless the travel is beyond our community. It also forbids the owning of telephones. This means that most communication inside our community depends on the use of our horse-drawn, wooden wheeled buggies. Farming also relies on horse-drawn implements and wagons.

Judging by the accidents caused in our community by the startle effect on animals, we can well imagine the horrors high decibel noise would inflict on us. For instance, just the other day, ice slid off a roof while an Amish farmer was hooking up two big draft-horses. They both bolted and one landed on its back in a ditch. No one is strong enough to hold back an eight foot high, ten foot long horse, weighing 2,000 pounds!

On another occasion, a dump truck dumped gravel and this noise caused a hitched team of horses to bolt. Such animals remain skittish and untrustworthy for years — while some never get over the shock. A horse pulling a buggy carrying parents with a young daughter sitting between them was startled by the sudden appearance of a car. When the driver of the car honked, the horse reacted instinctively by kicking back at what was behind it — striking the little girl in the head and causing her to bleed to death in her mother's arms...

* * *

Many Amish families have about thirty-five cows and heifers totaling approximately 22,000 cows and young stock in the threatened communities. Part of a day's work includes milking by hand, and children from about six years of age and up help with this and many other farm chores. Younger children are also often present in the barns. The physical safety of anyone

111

sitting next to the rear flank of a cow weighing up to 1,500 pounds is in extreme danger should the animal be startled by noise. The cow could kick or trample the milker and anyone else nearby.

* * *

We rely on the sale of milk for cheese-making and we have heard of the reduced production of milk by dairy cows in similarly affected areas. High decibel noise would impact the livelihood of all of us. However, jet fumes and fuel spills would be another hazard for those of us who produce organic vegetables and milk for sale.

Loud, low-flying bombers threaten not only our religion and our lives, but also sound a death-knell for our way of life. We are a self-reliant, tax-paying community not taking any government social security, subsidies, set aside programs or aid of any kind. However, we are asking in earnest that the United States Government send a group of people to see how we live and to conduct a scientific survey to answer our concerns.

If we are forced to leave the Kickapoo Valley region, who will buy our farms? Where could we go? Will we be left as prisoners here?

We are very concerned about our situation. We are also very sad about the threat to our farms because our love for our rural way of life is a spiritual value based on Scripture. We believe that the first and second verses, of the second chapter of Paul's First Epistle to Timothy, express our hearts' feeling:

"I exhort therefore, that, first of all supplications, prayers, intercessions and giving of thanks, be make for all men;

For kings and for all that are in authority; that we may lead a quiet and peaceable life in all godliness and honesty..."

The question is what will become of our heart's desire? Also our precious, God-given freedom that we have.

You surely have a home of your own. So, bearing this in mind, you would not want this to interrupt your peace — we are sure. The Golden Rule is, 'Do unto others as you would have them do unto you.' 'Love thy neighbor as thyself.'

With this in mind we fervently pray and trust that God will give you heart and feeling to consider our Heartfelt Plea to answer our many questions.

Sincerely,

Signed by over 500 members of the local congregations.

From Tranquillity, Farewell

AUGUST DERLETH

The afternoon of the October day was approaching the hour of sundown and twilight, and already the distances were lost in a pale, lavender haze. Along the ridge a stage moved steadily in a generally northeasterly direction, at a pace which suggested that its goal was not far distant, though no dwelling was in sight in all that wild country of hills and valleys. Still visible along the horizon to the southwest rose the Platte and Belmont Mounds, passed more than an hour ago — twin, rounded hills standing forth like dark, grave sentinels in a land of silence and strangeness, dominating the face of the earth at that place. An illusion of level land lay between the blue peaks and the ridge road, a tranquil country of high plateau and deep valleys, but at this hour the valleys were lost in the last sunlight lying in a soft pin and copper haze along their slopes, complimenting the colors of ivy, sumac, birch trees, and hazel brush which grew at the edge of every copse and thicket. In the ravines nearby, sunlight lay pooled and warm; a kind of shimmering, colorful and mystic, filled the air, but beyond, in the deep, wooded valleys between the ridges, the first dusk already flowered where sunlight and day were withdrawn.

August Derleth was regarded by many as Wisconsin's leading contributor to regional literature. This excerpt appears by arrangement with his family.

Home of the Manitou

O P A L A N I Y E   M I T K E M

Tourism promoters often let the phrase slip: God's Country. Of course, it is all the Creator's. S/He doesn't care if you don't believe. The lesser spirits may even feel sorry for you if you don't believe, but the Great Spirit is above all that.

Humans often wonder if the Creator favors certain locations or designates specific sites for interactions with mortals. Cynics find the notion of sacred place and sacred space to be an intellectual construct with no divine inspiration working on any level.

Yet, there are many among us — of all races and social standings — who repeatedly experience the Creator at a favorite spot. Many will not admit the real reason behind their outdoor forays. Many find transcendence, healing, and power in even the recollection of a sacred place.

What makes a sacred place, a holy land, a home of the Manitou?

It is more than scenic beauty, which abounds throughout the world despite our best efforts to pave paradise. It is more than age-old traditions of worship and meditation at religious sites.

Some spots allow us to see the handiwork of the Manitou, experience Manitou energy and, sometimes, even let us glimpse the Manitou. It can happen any place, but has a way of repeating itself at the sites of awe-inspiring natural beauty.

In North America we have many such awesome sites. Some might find Wisconsin lacking in these spectacular features. And perhaps there are not the bold, angry, or humorous strokes on the Wisconsin canvas that make for world class pilgrimage attractions.

The Manitou has been more gentle here, not flexing muscles or making points. Here the Manitou has built a lodge of many rooms. There are comfy spots. Front porch bluffs, womb-like coulees, soothing rivers, and tranquil lakes.

The Manitou doesn't play or tread angrily here in flyover country. No, the Manitou lives here.

You don't believe me? Well, visit the Woodland Bowl at Keshena for a Menominee powwow. You'll be in the Manitou's breast and will feel the heartbeat. Behold the bejeweled Apostle Islands as the morning mist lifts from Lake Superior. Nestle in the twists and turns of the Kickapoo River. Feast the eyes with an overlook of a sparkling Lake Michigan.

The challenge is not to find the Manitou. The challenge is to stumble onto a place where the Manitou can find you.

Once found, give thanks there often. Hold that place in your mind's eye. Become intimate with every nook and cranny. The Manitou has appointed you guardian of that place. Do your duty.

Opalaniye Mitkem is a community organizer and writes about social justice issues under a given English name. He is Munsee/Lenni Lenape and is studying eastern Algonquin shamanism.

Floyd

JERRY APPS

Floyd Jeffers lived across the road from our newly acquired Waushara County farm. We had bought the Coombes' place, a sandy, hilly piece of land that some of the better farmers in the community had deemed worthless.

Floyd came over almost every day the summer I worked on the shack, a 1912 granary that I was trying to convert into a cabin. He was old and bent, thin, almost frail, and leaned heavily on a walking stick. Floyd walked with a shuffle, but his eyes sparkled and his pointed face lit up when he talked. It was a slow drawl that neither went up nor down but continued on a single pitch.

I knew Floyd Jeffers since I was a boy growing up on a farm a couple of miles north of our newly acquired acres. But I had not known him well because he was not a party of the threshing, silo filling, corn shedding and wood sawing crews in our neighborhood. The neighbors thought that Floyd was a little peculiar. He was a bachelor who milked a few skinny Guernsey cows, grew a few acres of corn and owned mostly pasture land and woods.

Floyd was a voracious reader, reading several newspapers, many magazines and scores of books. Most farmers in our neighborhood didn't have much time for reading, except for maybe a farm paper and the weekly Waushara Argus that kept them apprised of local news. They thought that anyone who read as much as Floyd was lazy and wasn't much of a farmer.

Now, years later, Floyd came over to watch me work on the granary, and spin stories.

"How much you know about your new place?" Floyd asked one day.

"Not much," I confessed. I had known Weston Coombes and his mother since I was a kid, but I didn't know anything about their farm, which now belonged to my family and me.

"Know which white man settled your farm first?" Floyd asked.

"Nope, I don't," I said. This had not been a question I'd thought about. My single purpose that summer was making the old granary, with its gray weathered boards and leaky roof, into something livable.

"Name was Tom Stewart, from Rose, New York. Came here in 1867.

Got the land for nothin' because he was a Civil War veteran. Had to build a cabin. Had to farm some, too, as part of the deal."

I knew that several pioneers in this part of Waushara County had come from upper New York State, including Floyd's family who arrived more than 100 years ago. But I didn't know that a New Yorker had settled my farm.

Floyd went on. "Tom Stewart was Mrs. Coombes' father - she grew up on this place and lived most of her life here," Floyd said.

"Mrs. Coombes told stories about how her father broke this land with oxen and a breaking plow. Was mostly prairie land then. Some woods around the lakes. But mostly open prairie. Tall grass. Lots of wild flowers. She often talked about the wild flowers. Entire hillsides of wild flowers."

I told Floyd that I was interested in wild flowers, too, and was trying to key out the names of those I found on the farm.

"That's good," Floyd said, shaking his head up and down. "But take time to just look at them. Smell them, too. You don't need to know something's name to appreciate it. Some folks spend all their time naming and never get around to appreciating."

Floyd came over nearly every day that summer and each day was a lesson about the land and its people, although I didn't fully appreciate it at the time.

"You know that little country school down on the corner?" Floyd said one day when we sat under the black willow trees.

"Know it well," I said. "Went there for eight years."

"I went there, too," Floyd said with a smile. "Except I didn't finish eight grades, Pa needed me on the farm."

"Not like the town schools," I offered.

"Sure not. Know what made those country schools so important?"

"What was that?"

"Kids who went to those schools knew who they were. They knew where they were, too. Nothing more important than knowing who you are. Can't know that until you know where you are."

I must have looked puzzled, because Floyd continued.

"You grow up on a piece of land - you become a part of it. It becomes a part of you. When you go to a country school, you become a part of a community. The community becomes a part of you."

"Never thought of it that way," I said.

"Yup, when they closed all these little schools we lost something."

"Little farms are disappearing, too," I said. "Farm where I grew up has been divided into four parts. City folks are building houses on the land."

"Not a good thing," Floyd said, shaking his head. "Not a good thing. All this land going for houses with a few acres. Before you know it we won't have any open space."

I mentioned to Floyd about the farms west of here that had been sold and had become part of larger farms, some of them now more than a thousand acres.

"Not good," Floyd said. He was digging the end of his walking stick in the sand by his feet. "The bigger the farm, the less attachment the farmer has to his land. Land's more than a place to plant crops and try and make some money. Land is alive. Constantly changing. These 'modern' farmers test it, probe it, fertilize it, spray it, knock down the hills, fill in the valleys, drain the wet spots. Where will it end?"

"I'm sure I don't know," I said, trying to fully understand what Floyd was saying. At the time I was more interested in problems with my cabin project than hearing Floyd lamenting about what was happening to the land.

"The Indians have it right," Floyd said.

"How's that?"

"They say the land is sacred. They say if you take care of the land, the land will take care of you."

I wondered what Floyd was driving at. A couple of days later, Floyd returned. It was hot and humid, and I welcomed a break from sawing boards and pounding nails. We sat together, under the black willow trees to the west of the granary, not saying much of anything for a time. Then Floyd began.

"It starts with history. Got to help people become acquainted with their histories, their stories about connections to the land."

I must have looked puzzled, because Floyd stopped talking for an instant.

"Do you know what I'm saying?" he inquired.

"I think so," I replied. But I really didn't know what he was driving at.

Floyd continued, "Everyone has a connection to the land. Might be a couple of generations ago, but there's a connection."

"Guess you're right about that," I answered, still not really understanding.

"Help people see their connections to the land and maybe they'll treat it a little different," Floyd said. He leaned back in his chair and closed his eyes. For a moment, I thought he'd gone to sleep. Then his eyes snapped open. "Land's the most important thing we got. Most important thing," he said.

I had to be away from the farm for several weeks and didn't return until later in the summer. I expected Floyd to walk across the road when he saw my car in the yard. But he didn't come that day or the next either.

In Wild Rose for supplies, I asked about Floyd.

"Didn't you hear? Floyd died two weeks ago. Had a blood clot in his leg and it got worse," the clerk at the Co-op said.

I sat under the black willow trees alone that afternoon, thinking about what this old farmer, who everyone thought a little strange, had shared with me. I let his ideas roam around in my mind as I sat under the trees, feeling a soft breeze from the southwest, and listening to the quiet rustle of leaves. Now, many years later, I still think about Floyd's ideas. They seem as fresh today as they were then, and as difficult for many of us to understand.

Jerry Apps has written extensively about rural Wisconsin and is the author of many books on these themes, including Barns of Wisconsin.

An Eleven-Year Old Summer

GAIL RICHARDSON

Sometimes we forget about the precious things God gives. Computers, reports, lessons, schedules, deadlines and hundreds of other things grab our attention and time. It has been so long since we spent time with anything that didn't require programming, printing, stirring, fixing, greasing or welding. We can't remember a day that wasn't spent taking care of all the stuff we accumulate.

Last summer I found a wonderful way to take care of this problem of not appreciating God's world. For two days I had the company of an eleven-year old boy who wasn't content to play Nintendo for 18 hours a day. My nephew, Andrew, came to the farm to help with the haying but also with great hope for time to explore. Between loads of hay I was blessed to have an eleven-year old boy bring adventure to our river bottom.

We stepped carefully in the tall grass near a low spot in the pasture that had become a catch basin from the many inches of rain we had received. Computers and electronics were forgotten as we explored God's creation.

Andrew crouched near the water's edge and delighted in catching the tiny half-inch frogs he scooped up easily with dirty hands. His leather gloves were left behind while he touched and poked the muddy edges of the pond. He balanced easily on the dead tree branches that gave him a better view of the pond and also a better position to grab blue-green dragonflies skittering across.

There is something about dogs and eleven-year old boys that go together. It didn't take long for Roxie (our Border Collie cow dog) to find that Andrew was strong enough to fling sticks to the middle of the pond again and again until both were tired of the game. "That a girl, Roxie! Go get it!" And go she would! It's a wonder that any water was left in the pond by the end of the day.

These summer days gave an element of mystery for Andrew. He had to figure out if the big splash he heard behind him was really a big fish or a result of a grandpa who loved to tease. He talked to his older cousin about that big fish in the pond. Of course his cousin grinned and assured Andrew there was a big fish there. Andrew hoped to catch that big fish, but deep down knew that the big splash was from Grandpa. Eleven-year old boys can still take the time to dream about the wonderful possibility of catching such a prize.

In the hay wagon we talked. "My mom caught the biggest fish yesterday." He explained the art of fishing for perch, blue gills, and small mouth bass. He told me about getting up early and what a great day they had together as a family on a fishing trip. He shared with me that he liked to make homemade noodles with his dad. Later, once we got all the dirt off his hands, he showed me he could really handle himself in the kitchen as easily as the pond.

I was glad for this chance to stop for a while in the business of controlling nature. That call of an eleven-year-old boy, "Hey! Look what I found!" excited me to look at the next bit of treasure. His smiling dirt-streaked face made me want to linger at the pond and give praise. I think it is necessary for our souls to find awe at the details that each half-inch frog, dragon fly, big stick and tall grass exhibits — the sheer wonder of it all.

Gail Richardson farms with husband Ron near Benton, Wisconsin. She writes of farm life and conducts a clown ministry in her rural church. This essay is excerpted from Clippings, *the newsletter of the Church's Center for Land and People.*

Wisconsin by Night:
Me and the Hex

STEPHEN M. BORN

I've come to believe that an addiction to trout fishing must be genetically encoded. And nowhere was that sport more exciting to pursue than in the mountainous country dissected by big brawling rivers of the West. A Midwesterner, I moved West as a young man. Like a zealous convert to a new cause, I transferred my allegiance and affection to the scale, grandeur, open spaces and angling of the Western landscape. My appreciation for flatland diminished daily.

But career options and family considerations intervened, and in 1969, having completed my dissertation in the Great Basin, I returned to Wisconsin to begin my career at the university in Madison. On more than a few dark winter evenings I lamented my severance from the rushing trout-filled rivers and streams of Oregon, California, Montana and Wyoming. The small, unenergetic, pasture creeks and streams of southern Wisconsin didn't look very interesting or romantic, although I knew trout lived there. There was no way to foresee the love that would blossom over the next three decades with Wisconsin's land, waters, and trout.

An old Department of Natural Resources biologist friend who I worked and traveled with around the state, and who always reminded me of Mark Trail — the pipe-smoking outdoor sage of the daily comics — was forever extolling the diversity of Wisconsin — from the reborn northern forests through the "tension zone" to the deciduous woodlands of the south; from the Father of Waters on our western border to the shores of Lakes Superior and Michigan; from the glaciated terrain of most of the state to the driftless "coulee country" of southwestern Wisconsin, where I would later become a devotee of the hundreds of miles of challenging creeks. I was unimpressed. It took years for the subtle character of the Wisconsin landscape to win me over. Or more accurately, to open my eyes.

The trout fishing had something to do with that. My first Wisconsin trout foray grew out of an invitation from a friend to experience what I was assured is the zenith of trout angling — fishing the nighttime Hexagenia mayfly hatch. These largest members of the mayfly family burrow, subsist, and grow in soft, muddy sediment throughout their one to two year life cycles, emerging into winged adults during their June-July "coming out" party. After a few days resting in streamside vegetation, the adult "Hex" insect crawls out of its skin one last time, to complete its mating and egg-laying acts. I'd been told that every big trout in a river or stream with Hex mayflies awaited this transformation, as did every angler worthy of that title of trout fisher.

A few days later, I found myself being dropped off in the early evening at a bridge over the Mecan River in central Wisconsin's sand country. We would rendezvous there after the evening's excitement had run its course. Following my friend's instructions, I headed a quarter mile upstream to prepare myself for the grand event. It took almost an hour to slog through the mucky swamps, stumbling and tripping through tag alders, finally reaching my destination. It was a humid evening and sweat was pouring off my face, when the mosquitoes arrived. Slipping through a quagmire of mud, fending off mosquitoes and then bats, in the pitch black of night — I fumbled with a flashlight to get rigged up for this sublime experience.

I began to hear the sound of fish feeding in the darkness, but locating them and casting to them seemed impossible. The memory of those glorious days astream "out West" crossed my mind. After a futile hour of flailing the water with the big dry fly imitation, with a net result of one meager six inch brown trout, I began working my way back to the prescribed meeting place — through the hip deep mud and squadrons of mosquitoes. As I met up with my enthusiastic friend, I vowed this would be my first and my last experience of this type — that this crude, sweaty activity in the dark of a Wisconsin swamp was too far removed from the visual aesthetic experience I associated with my pursuit of trout.

Many years have passed through my net since that summer evening. The groundwater-fed streams flowing through lush wetland complexes — the Mecan, the White, the Tomorrow-Waupaca, Black Earth Creek, and many others — now rank among my most cherished Wisconsin places. Every watershed, every stretch of stream conjures up a memory. And despite my attachment to things seen (visual observations being essential in the training of a geologist), the eerie loneliness and sensory experience of night fishing has captivated me.

On balmy Wisconsin summer evenings, I anticipate being waist deep in another stream as the sun slips inexorably below the horizon. The drive to the stream is a worthy prelude to an evening of trout. To the observant eye with a bit of geologic training, the fingerprints of the Ice Age are beautifully displayed across the landscape. Of the streams I fish, the Mecan quickly comes to mind, their headwaters on the eastern side of a northerly glacial moraine. These streams flow southeast into the Fox River drainage and ultimately into Lake Michigan.

After a short hike, I'm wading upstream to my planned nighttime "beat". The water glides past me, cooling my legs as I wait with excitement. I share my expectations for the evening with patient red-wing blackbirds. Will there be a hatch? The darkness deepens, but no Hex duns appear. As I listen to the sound of brush breaking not far from the stream — a deer? - I ponder leaving, a victim of the fickle behavior of insects.

But suddenly I feel something whizzing past my head - and then another. Hex spinners! Within minutes the air is filled with these giant female insects winging their way upstream seeking out a seemingly predestined reach of stream for their final act of egg-laying. The drone of the mayfly air force intensifies, as they pass only feet above my head, intent only upon procreation. Soon they are adrift on the water. Every square foot of stream seems occupied by twitching, struggling Hex spinners. I hear fish gorging all along this watery conveyor-belt buffet.

The fishing is explosive, but short-lived. Within half an hour, the stream is still, and while a few wild brown trout have felt the sting of my hook and the touch of my hand, most of the trout population has eased back to their lairs and resting places, sated with a buggy smorgasbord.

Back at the truck, my gear safely stored, I reward myself with a beer. My pipe smoke chases away a few straggler mosquitoes as I digest the evening and contemplate the drive home. The West — it's still a grand setting and I love chasing trout there every year. But Wisconsin is my home, an environment that I know and feel as much as I see.

Steve Born is a professor of planning and environmental studies at UW-Madison; chair of the National Resources Board of Trout Unlimited; and coauthor of Exploring Wisconsin Trout Streams: the Angler's Guide *(from which this essay is adapted).*

Sketches of Winter Along the Manitowish River

MARY BURNS

Winter solstice today. A fog rises and shrouds the white marshes. Snow, compressed by consecutive 40 degree days, sags underfoot. Last week it was cold, and like a healing wound, the ice had slowly edged out over the water. The jagged white coverings had stitched over the black water during the nights, almost sealing the current below its sheets. But now with the unseasonable warmth, the river has new strength, and the ice retreats to the river banks.

The north country winter spreads forth from early November, and blows its icy breath into late March. The northern residents — plant, animal, and human — adapt to various cold weather lifestyles. Here along the Manitowish River our woodpile is deep and high, and usually the snow is too. Both provide insurance against the cold.

The scant eight hours of sunlight during the solstice lacks the strength to burn off the fog. Today the balmy air does not sweep keenly into the lungs with every breath. But there is a bright spot. The woodpile goes down more slowly than in winters past.

Later in the evening, behind the trunks of white pines, the moon rises with a milky glowing aura. Snow covered fields lay open in the moonlight, etched with tracks and tall grasses. Even in the brightness, the stars surface in the night sky. Orion's belt shines in the southeast, and Polaris steadfastly points to the pole. The temperature has dropped, and the air now bites sharply. A cold, radiating clarity spreads through the darkness. Perhaps in this season of the winter solstice, the beauty truly is of the night. It curls itself around the northlands in a blanket almost 16 hours long. In this night, the spirit of Christmas is born.

* * *

Stepping into the ski bindings, I wedge the three pins into the tip of the soles and clamp them tight. With the pole straps looped around my wrists,

125

I slide forward. Kick and glide, kick and glide, shuffle through the deep snow, then glide again where the snow is packed and firm, I slip down the little hill near the house to the edge of the marsh, and angling the skis along the bank, drop down onto the ice. Stems of tan sedges protrude from their hummocks and wave well above the snow. Just inside the entangling, vile clusters of alder, the rabbit tracks are thick.

The early January sun shines palely in the late afternoon, its warmth not exceeding 10 degrees nor slowing the brisk westerly wind. Gusts fling the new snow high into the air like white ghosts, eddying and whirling above the river. A thin strand of tracks crosses and re-crosses the river, a coyote's recording of its nighttime journey.

* * *

In late January on a section of the Manitowish several miles upstream from our home, the snow lays deep on the high bank, and a winter quiet hugs the land. Pines wear a heavy coat of snow, while birch and aspen stand naked. A gust of wind rifles through the red oaks, rustling the withered brown leaves like paper socks hung out to dry. Below, the river ripples swift and alive in the cold. The open water draws in the animals. Their trails track across the forest into the thickets, to the cedar glade, and to the river. This is a deer highway in the snow, where they seek out shelter, food, water.

I snowshoe through the timber to reach the river's edge. A splash startles me, and I look upstream to see the reddish brown head of a deer bobbing in the rapids. It holds its muzzle high above the water. The deer swims across the river while the current steadily pushes it downstream closer to me. Reaching the bank, it climbs through the sandy snow, and disappears into the woods. I snowshoe upstream to find its tracks blended in with many others. Following the deer, I add my tracks to the calligraphy of the winter trails.

* * *

A few eagles remain in February in this same section of the river which stays open all winter dark and inky against the white banks. The eagles usually perch in pines along the open water scouting for a flicker of life beneath the surface. They also feed on road kills or other carrion, leading a glorified vulture's life, but winter survival requires the seizing of opportunities, not polite formalities.

An immature eagle, mottled white and brown, stretches its wings broadly, glides from its white pine perch above the rapids, and follows the river downstream.

Sometimes the eagles gather in groups. One day we counted eleven in trees along a rocky stretch of water where the current is swift. But most often we spot one or two. In southern Wisconsin they congregate in groups of 50 or more, but there the winter ice isn't so thick, and open water predominates. Here, on bigger lake waters, ice fishermen occasionally leave fish on the ice, and the eagles will come in and dine.

* * *

On a late March night, the northern lights wash across the night sky. For hours, these polar lights flare and arc southward. The following evening, a great horned owl's low call resonates across the marsh — a call to arise, the warmth is coming. On the third night, the river below our house breaks its bonds of ice and flows freely. The months of encasement are gone in a burst of groans and cracklings.

When I awake the next morning I feel a new freedom, as if the skin of winter's chill has been lifted away. Two days later, we trudge through the field of old snow and launch the canoes. To be on the river again and feel the current tugging at the bow must be close to the feeling of wings in flight.

Thick ice covers the marshes and juts out over the river. We wind through the river oxbows alongside layers of ice built up over the space of a winter. It feels like we are on an archeological exploration through the stratums. Sometimes this white armor cracks and melts, and slips softly into the river. Other ice sheets break and fall into the water with a startling splash, their weight striking deeply into the water. Then they bob up and join the flotilla drifting downstream.

When we poke at the shelves of ice, they dissolve into three-inch shards and pierce the water as they fall like a hundred needle points. The ice is rotting. What once had appeared white and pristine is littered with bits of soil, bark, vegetation, and flies. These insects are similar to May flies and seem to be emerging from the layers of ice.

Cold seeps from the ice and rolls onto the water — It is a chill burn of the dark of winter, holding on here in the warm spring sun. Water drips in a constant pattering off the underside of the ice that cantilevers out over the river, as if a small rainstorm had brewed in the icy caverns. The pattering reminds us of spring peepers that will soon be chorusing their arrival. The ice continues to melt and fall off into the river like a small receding glacier, taking winter with it.

Soon the red-winged blackbirds will arrive. They usually appear on

March 21st, the spring solstice, staking out their ancestral territories in the marshes bordering the river. Along with their home-coming, the snow will begin to deflate, collapsing and compressing back into water. Early evening fogs will rise from the marshes, lifting like emerging butterflies, as if the winter was hovering between life and death.

By spring, solstice eagles will be incubating their eggs high in the pines. White weasels will turn brown again to match the newly exposed soil. Does will grow heavier with fawns. The river will break, and then percolate in its spring migration into the Flambeau River, then to the Chippewa, the Mississippi, and finally the Gulf. And we will continue to explore our understanding of this place, our accountability to the generations that were here before us, and those to come.

Mary Burns is a writer who lives in the Manitowish River area.

A Journey Through the Medicine Wheel in Wisconsin

ANNE STEVENS

We are newly arrived in Wisconsin. Travelers from the warm sands and shimmering waters of Florida. I have returned to a land of four seasons reminiscent of my childhood in the woodlands of New Jersey. There are fewer trees here, and the stretch of rolling hills seem like great waves reaching for some distant shore. In the morning mist I can almost see a joining of land and sea on the horizon, and then remember; it is farmland merging into farmland, and the distant 'lighthouse' becomes a silo again.

Not long after we moved here, we saw an eagle circling above "our" land. His place on the sacred wheel is the east and his presence may signal the dawn of new beginnings. Able to soar above the pull of circumstances, eagle joins heaven and earth; spirit and matter. We are reminded by his presence to seek clarity of direction by renewing our sacred vision and purpose. When our spirits are unfettered, we like eagle, can soar unencumbered, and feel the wind beneath our wings.

The morning sun migrates to the south, the next place of touching upon the wheel, speaking of beauty and the blossom of summer in our lives. Life passionately bursts forth in a rush and fervor to live and beget life, and here, in the country, it is never in small measures. Acre upon acre of dandelions, the 'lion's tooth', disappear in the distance like a yellow brick road in search of the fabled city of Oz. Clusters of small, yellow butterflies congregate in our driveway and the county roads, and china bugs, not unlike lady bugs, clump on the screens in great masses. Birds sing, frogs croak, fat, yellow and black spiders spin tales. Everything pushes and pulls in a great race to live life to the fullest.

It is here, too, that the child dwells, reminding us of our own inner child and of simplicity, playfulness, and love. I have recently 'journeyed' to the south becoming a mother once again. With eyedropper and formula I am nursing five, small, gentle rabbits. They are becoming robust and soon I will need to release them into the wild. The simple act of mothering them nudges out the caring heart in both my daughter and myself, which sometimes gets misplaced in our busy lives. Thus we, in turn, are nurtured and nourished by the innocence and trust of these tiny creatures.

The sun journeys next into the west; sunset, the light turning within. It is the autumn of our lives as well. I watch the fluttering leaves and acorns as they carpet and cobblestone the forest floor. Anytime we find ourselves in a place of simple reflection or deep introspection, we dwell in the west. The eagle teaches us of the height of our being; owl takes us into the depth, a voyage into the unknown. To retreat, as hibernating bear teaches, we must leave all behind as gracefully as the earth offering her golden harvest upon the alter of her being. It is a time of yielding and movement. Flame-colored trees dance like gypsies to the music of the wind. Geese call and I yearn to join them in their flight. Corn stalks turn bronze and the night air breathes frost on the pumpkin and vine.

Winter is birthed in the north, and its hallmark is wisdom born of life's experiences. It is night, offering respite and renewal. I stand in awe of the great sweep of stars in the dark sky. Once again I see the Milky Way, hidden from my eyes for many years by burning city lights. I meet my old friend, the constellation Orion the Hunter. He and I were introduced by an elementary school teacher and I often seek his reassuring presence. I see too, Taurus the bull, and the Pleiades seven sisters who cling to Taurus' back. It is a humbling experience for me to glimpse the vastness of the universe and be aware of my own gift of life.

I love the snow-laden days when earth and sky are of the same color. I, a 50 year old child can lie on the earth and imagine falling into the sky; into a land where snow people live their wintery lives. When it is time to leave, I somersault back into my body lying inert in the snow. It is a shaman's journey for the young at heart. Winter is both pristine and peaceful and in its overwhelming stillness, I have never felt more alive. It is a time of solitude and peace; it is where all things come to rest. Here, the promise of spring is held in the wise and caring heart of the earth until it, like ourselves, emerges into spring and the dawn of new beginnings.

Anne Stevens teaches sacred earth traditions near Mineral Point. She has written short stories on spiritual healing.

Up North On the South Shore

WARREN NELSON

"When I first came to this land, I was not a wealthy man. But the land was sweet and good, and I did what I could." (old folk song)

I.

When I first came to Wisconsin, gas was 49.9 cents, and on a 1978 spring day I drove up north from Mazomanie. I had never seen northern Wisconsin. I had a gig with the Lost Nation String Band at Archie's Supper Club in Washburn. The day before, Bruce Burnside, the mandolin player, stopped by and we unfolded a state map on the car hood and he pointed me around the Bayfield Peninsula with his index finger. Going up and down County Road C showing me the pine-lined way to Cornucopia from Washburn and where the turn-off to his place was. I noticed right off a lot of green national forest squares on the map and a lack of marked roads and the strange name Chequamegon and a bunch of islands I had never heard of. And I remember staring a good long while at County Trunk C.

Poof and proof — here's to destiny. Twenty years later I live in the pines just off County C, west of Washburn, on the pine-lined way to Cornucopia — leave my bones here when my eyes go dark.

There is considerable debate (or ought to be) as to where northern Wisconsin officially begins. Living near Madison, I would hear, "I'm going to a convention tomorrow up north in Stevens Point." Or take notice of the billboard on U.S. 51 that declares Portage "The Gateway To The North!" We have to give Portage a wide berth on that claim because of the ancient importance of the portage between the Wisconsin and Fox River waterways, the oldest big easy from the Mississippi to the Great Lakes. But I don't think so now. It doesn't hold twentieth century water.

The whole question of where "up north' begins is worthy of a seminar in this our sesquicentennial year. It should be held up north. That means anywhere north of U.S. Highway 2. Everything south of Highway 2 is Confederate.

Some would border "up north" at the old southern pine line, where the great virgin forests began their stands. The state by the DNR's hand draws two fishing lines. The Largemouth and Smallmouth Bass Management Zones zig-zag from Lake Michigan on Highway 29 to 64 and then Highway 27 north to 70 and then west to the St. Croix. The Muskie and Northern Pike line cuts clean, takes Highway 10 from the eastern water border to the western, filleting Wisconsin in half. Then there is the "get-shafted line" according to a social service worker friend of mine who says Highway 29 is where the money stops coming up from Madison. But mine is more a spiritual question.

I thought for a long time that "up north" officially begins when you cross the historically famous Mason-Bibon Line on Highway 63 north of Grandview. But I am now set on Highway 2 and will cut you into tiny lots if you ever dare debate me on the subject.

II.

"Car wash at the coal dock!" Kathy calls her mom Patsy on Easter Sunday afternoon. The sky is gray — it's a big blow, small craft gale warnings for the south shore. Nobody in Washburn is open for business, everybody's cruising. There must be twenty-five cars lined up to drive around the big gravel pile to the coal dock's end where waves are roaring over the new timbers. Chequamegon is having its loud angry say. The waves at the dock corners meet but you never know which by the wind is a breaker. Wash your car one side as you slowly drive by taking your turn. Holman is here with his muddy van. We're really here to be rebaptized by the power of the waters of Mother Superior. Some circle twice.

Alone in my Ford Escort confessional booth, I roll up the window — if the bay is so wild at this harbor in the lee of the Apostle Islands, what is it like out on the open lake, beyond Outer Island? I sing an old song of mine to myself — "There's enough darkness in a man... my God, out here it stands up in your bones. And rolls your soul like a stone in the wash...on the banks of Outer Island...at the banks of Outer Island."

I go around again. This is the old merchandise dock built at Washburn's founding by the railroad and by the Minneapolis grain barons, autumn 1883. Washburn is the Washburn of Cadwallader C., one term governor of Wisconsin and later defector to Minnesota when he took ownership of St. Anthony's Falls — the Washburn of the Washburn-Crosby Company Flour Mills — WCCO Radio of Minneapolis. General Mills-Wheaties. Cheerios-Betty Crocker — the first grain elevator on Lake Superior stood just south of this dock which reaches 550 feet out in the lake. It is 180 feet wide. The huge elevator, torn down in 1911, was put up by 1100 men in four and a half months, from the first brick to the last shaft and pulley. Buffalo, Cleveland and Washburn were in those flush old times neighbors of the water. Now it's just us at the car wash in the spray of Chequamegon Bay.

III.

I come here most every morning all year — some days to sit an hour, some days to drive through, some days to face the winds, to stand to. Two days after the blow, I'm looking out on a sheet of water that barely ripples. In one small boat floats the soul of a fisherman. North towards Bayfield, the brownstone coast is gold in the morning light, diminishing into a two-mile Mediterranean white-sand beach that spreads from the mouth of the Sioux River. Madeline Island, spiritual home yet of the Ojibwa people, ghost outpost of the French fur trade and Jesuit missions and now ice-road and ferry-ride home to locals and the resorting summer rich, appears to float above the water in the blue distance. Long Island snakes its sand towards the longshore ore-dock city of Ashland, and long to the south the slough at the bottom of the bay is wet with spring, with bird whistle, gull screeching and swan trumpeting. The Penokee Mountain Range of Michigan is way over there, in back and over it all.

Oldtimers up north on the south shore call Lake Superior "the pond." The largest body of freshwater in the world — "the pond" — those of us who call the Chequamegon Bay area home know we live north of northern Wisconsin.

In the faces of the commercial fishermen of Bayfield, born to their boats, I have seen the long eye. And the new day that motors out before dawn, out of Chequamegon Bay, out into the open lake.

Gitchee-Gumee, over your faces an ancient peace glides,
Cold-waved, wind-spread,
The tides of a June day-breaking.

Across the bay from the Ashland overlook, I see the townsite of Washburn where for keeps I have landed. An Illinois family jumps excitedly out of their van, pointing across the water. "Do you live here?" I nod. "Is that Canada?" "Yes it is".

Warren Nelson is producer and artistic director of the Lake Superior Big Top Chautauqua. He met Elvis twice!

A Room Without A View

ANONYMOUS

Wetland smells penetrate the concrete walls to tell me that it is spring in Wisconsin. An unseen marsh entertains my mind with visions of ducks, frogs, and red-winged blackbirds rocking gently on cattails.

The exercise area affords us a view of fences, razor wire, and a grassy berm. This is all I know of rural Wisconsin. This is to be my home for the rest of my life.

What I know of nature I know from my grandfather. He was Mississippi born and came up to work in the factories of Milwaukee during the war. He took me fishing on Lake Michigan's breakwaters and piers.

Grandfather showed us the bounty of backyard gardens. He'd say, "Look, smell that dirt — there's life in that there dirt." But for him and his stories of the South we would have grown up thinking food came from Kohls and milk from convenience stores.

He told incredible stories to children on the front stoops of Milwaukee. Black men who owned and milked cows. Black children who rode ponies and mules. Uncles bringing gifts of heavy stringers of catfish. Grandmothers who picked peaches off their own backyard trees. We thought these stories stranger than the Land of Oz — yet it seemed like a promised land.

Where is that land? Where is the place in nature for a people ripped from their natural place? The marsh is silent.

Dark species in a pale northern European sea, are we invasive exotics like those dumped from the ballast of foreign freighters? Are these blossoming prisons our legacy to the land? The marsh is silent.

During a movement for health care treatment I savor the cheap thrill of two correctional officers sharing memories of a fishing trip. I am invisible to them, but I share the sunlight off that distant lake. Children giggle on a beach. Women fuss with hair in a breeze. Men hold full bellies and caress cold beers.

The wild within me leaves the body. My wild soars to that lake, cavorts with fish and eagles, and splashes with children too young to hate.

A push from behind brings me back within the walls. Out on the marsh my wild breaks the silence with a howl.

Anonymous is an inmate at a Wisconsin correctional facility.

Learning to be a Wisconsin Writer

HARVEY M. JACOBS

When I first received the invitation to contribute to this anthology, my reaction was "Me!? A Wisconsin writer?"

To understand my relationship to the Wisconsin landscape you need to start with the famous Steinberg cover for The New Yorker, the one where the map of the United States is pictured from the Manhattan-centric perspective of a dyed-in-the-wool New Yorker. In the picture's foreground are the details of "the city," then back a bit is New Jersey and then not much lies beyond that until California looms in the distance. A vision of America without a middle that exists or matters.

I am a first generation American raised on the East Coast — as a child in Pittsburgh, PA and a teenager in the New York metropolitan area. I went to college in Buffalo, and after college lived in New England (Vermont to be exact). By the late 1970s, with a new baby in hand, my spouse and I moved back to New York State for me to attend graduate school at Cornell University. We were in and on a landscape that made sense — my in-laws were a hour and a half drive to the northwest, my parents five hours to the southeast. The rest of my wife's family were three hours to the northeast. When we thought about a college teaching position that would follow my graduate studies, we assumed/hoped it would be either in New York State or even more preferably rural, upper New England. Ours was a world of mixed forests, lush greens, explosive fall colors, mountains (Catskills, Adirondacks, Green and White), and the foothills that led to the mountains. The settled rural landscape of upstate New York was one of towns and villages past their prime, with peeling paint, and oftentimes histories forgotten.

The Midwest — through literature, culture and/or politics — wasn't a conscious part of how I understood the world. (I hadn't read The Little House on the Prairie books as a child, and I had only traveled to Chicago once, without much of a lasting image). And even where the Midwest was a part of my consciousness, Wisconsin as a distinct place wasn't even on the map — just like Steinberg's depiction.

For me at the time the upper mid-west was, if anything, a joke, a funny story. Garrison Keiller's radio show was in its early days then. On most Saturday nights, we would get together for a pot-luck dinner with a fami-

135

ly who had children our children's age (there were two now). When Garrison told his Lake Wobegon stories we roared. Or at least three of the four us did. The wife of the other couple often sat on the sofa stone faced. When we asked her what was wrong — why wasn't she laughing? She looked at us, and with all, seriousness, said "you don't get it, this isn't a joke!" She had grown up outside of the Twin Cities.

I share with you this background, because you need to know what I had as a framework to judge Wisconsin by when I arrived. I arrived in Wisconsin in the summer of 1984, from a single academic year teaching in a small college near Spokane, Washington. I had been here only once before, for my job interview. For several days in April I experienced Madison through a steady rain.

I didn't know how to read the landscape of what was now my new home. My first impressions were that it was too monochromatic and too flat. During that first summer my wife and I went out for a lazy summer afternoon canoe ride on Lake Wingra (the smallest of Madison's four lakes). We paused in the middle of the lake. Susan looks at me, and with a sweep of her hand says "you know what Madison needs?" I wondered what was on her mind, this person I had dragged across the country twice in one year, to land her in a place neither of us really knew anything about. "A small mountain right about there" (as she pointed to the southwest view from the lake). I knew what she meant.

But my work at the university soon started taking me out and about through the state. I teach land use and environmental policy, with a special focus on the policy alternatives available to sub-state governmental units (counties, cities, villages, and townships). As land use and environmental change are hot topics almost everywhere in the state, I never want for opportunities to travel within the state. As I traveled, I began my education. I began to move away from my inability to understand what was around me, and to only be able to compare it to that which I knew.

What I have found (and am finding) is a physical and cultural landscape different than anything I knew, and wholly captivating on its own terms. The place that most makes sense to me, given my background, is the driftless area of southwest Wisconsin. The first time I took a student group on a field trip to the region I had to pull the van over to the side of the road for ten minutes. I was crying. Here was a landscape that made visceral sense. A landscape of hills and valleys, a landscape of old settled communities, run down, out of the way, and forgotten. A landscape where people refused to give up, and in fact a landscape which allowed people to make and remake a semi-independent vision of how life could be lived with balance and in touch with nature.

When I can slip away, the other place that captures my heart is Madeline Island. A tip of land off the northern coast of the state, it harkens back to a time pre-modern in its rhythms. Since you can only get there by ferry, here you find a land and people whose life is lived several breaths slower than the rest of us. Camping in the state park, I have had the magical experience of waking in the middle of the night to find the sky aglow with the northern lights, dancing away in a light show that puts to shame any rock group stadium set. And then in the day there is the pleasure of wandering the shore of Lake Superior with its crystal clear, cold waters and a quiet so complete as to let all of the noise spill out of my ears.

But if the driftless area and Madeline Island are the most endearing parts of the state for me, because they are the easiest for me to understand and relate to, it is some of the other areas that I learn from. I have become sensitive to the subtle changes in landscape form and color as I drive out from Madison and head west, north, east or south. What first struck me as monochromatic and flat, I now see for itself. When I was in college in Buffalo studying in an architectural school, I was introduced to the work of Frank Lloyd Wright. He had several buildings in the city which I enjoyed walking by; I appreciated them for their obvious originality and inspiration. The use of muted, natural materials, and the low slung lines each building a distinctive work by the famed architect. Now that I live in southern Wisconsin, I understand the sources of his inspiration.

And then there are the small, quiet communities, where the farms leading into are well-kept and proud. The small cities and villages — such as Baraboo, Richland Center, River Falls — where the pride of place is nearly shouted from the rooftops. I'm not a big sports fan, never have been. But traveling to these communities to meet with local officials and citizen groups, makes me understand the pride of place that shows up in Madison during the year as part of the high school athletic competitions. You come from here, and you really do care to represent your community well, because you really have a community and it matters.

As part of my teaching, I introduce students to the concept of bioregionalism. Bioregionalism is rooted in the idea of a bioregion which one set of authors say "refers to a geographical terrain and a terrain of consciousness — to a place and the ideas that have developed about how to live in a place. Within a bioregion the conditions that influence life are similar and these in turn have influenced human occupancy." While technically Wisconsin is several bioregions, it also can function as one "terrain of consciousness." Wisconsin, as I've come to learn, is a place of pride — pride in its traditions, pride in its people, and pride in and for the land. While it is a slow process, I am proud to be becoming a Wisconsin writer.

Harvey Jacobs is a professor in the Department of Urban and Regional Planning, UW-Madison. He is the editor of Who Owns America?

The Blue Canoe

GEORGE VUKELICH

I went into the marshes the other day, and for the first time since last Fall, I had the Blue Canoe with me. No fishing gear. No fishing companion. Just the Blue Canoe. And one paddle.

In the canefield of river willow, the canoe lay like a fish in a woven creel, helpless and out of its element, calculating the distance to life but unable to bridge it.

I pushed the paddle into the muck and leaned into it.

God, I could almost hear Gordie Sussman wincing: Never use the paddle as a pole- if you need a pole, use a pole.

The paddle blade came up, creamy with muck and smelling of marsh. Not rank or gross, just smelling of marsh.

Three pushes more and we floated free of the tangle and into open water. I rested the paddle across the gunwales and stayed on my knees.

Daylight in the swamp, you could hear the voices saying. Daylight in the swamp. There was the vision of Deacon Davis, the Arkansas Stump Jumper, announcing dawn to the whole platoon in the tightened tones that sounded like guitar strings, and then throwing back his head and keening: "W-a-a-a-y—b-a-c-k—i-n—t-h-e—h-i-i-i-l-l-s."

No one had ever said, "Daylight in the swamp" to you before Deacon. All the years you were growing up and The Old Man woke you to go fishing or hunting, he just gripped your ankle as you slept, and pretty soon you wakened gently, and he was always dressed and saying softly: Time to go. Now you do the same thing to Vince and he wakes up the very way you did.

The canoe seemed to sniff out the main current and nosed its way into the channel.

It moved past the depths, where, not too many weeks back, the big buck deer had trotted down the snow-covered ice, never seeing you until the last moment.

It moved past the shallows, where, not too many weeks ahead, the spawning carp will thrash and explode, never seeing you at all.

It moved past the pussy willow clump where the catkins clung to the branches like resting caterpillars.

And there, beyond the pussy willows, washed into the shore, was the dead animal.

It seemed big as a beaver, big as a dog. I shuddered as I stared at it, but the shock of seeing it was not as great as the shock of realizing what it was.

Spread-eagled, on its back, bloated almost beyond recognition. It was huge as a hog, yet its claws, its teeth were those of a rodent.

Muskrat, I said out loud. Muskrat, what happened to you?

And slowly, yet of a sudden, it was as if I could hear an answer to my question.

Death happened to me, came the answer. Look at me closely, paddler. It will also happen to you.

I shuddered again. Then I just looked. And looked.

"Ma Nature," Steady would smile. "You better take notes. She's gonna ask questions."

There seemed to be a rip, a tear in the muskrat's belly as though something had been working on it, picking on it.

Hugh Percy always insisted that turtles got around to most dead things in the marshes eventually, kind of tidying up so it didn't get to be a cesspool.

"Death enters through the belly," Carlos Castaneda had written in *A Separate Reality*, "it enters right through the gap of will."

He was writing about men, humans, and perhaps that only applied to humans.

"Muskrats or millionaires," Steady insists, "it's all the same. Down here, it's all under Ma's rules."

"After all," Steady argues, "is the most natural thing in this world to be belly-up in a marsh, or belly-up in a mausoleum?"

Every part of nature, Henry David Thoreau observed, teaches that the passing away of one life is the making room for another. In Walden he wrote:

"The skeleton which at first excites only a shudder in all mortals, becomes at last not only a pure but a suggestive and pleasing object to science. The more we know of it, the less we associate it with any goblin of our imaginations. The longer we keep it, the less likely it is that any such will come to claim it. We discover that the only spirit which haunts it is a universal intelligence which has created it in harmony with all nature. Science never saw a ghost, nor does it look for any, but it sees everywhere the traces, and it is itself the agent, of a universal intelligence."

When I left the muskrat, it wasn't a lonely marsh anymore. The Blue Canoe was still empty, but I had company. Henry David. And Ma. And Steady Eddy.

"All the heavies," Steady likes to say.

On the way back, out of a clear blue sky, there was a hawk feather on the water and you could almost hear Augie Derleth.

At the garage, over coffee, Hugh Percy figured the feather probably came from a red-tail. I think he's half right. A red-tail probably dropped it.

The late George Vukelich was noted for his column and Wisconsin Public Radio show, "North Country Notebook." He created memorable conversation on social and ecological issues in the setting of the Three Lakes American Legion Bar. This essay was selected by his family.

Winter's Holy Ground

MIRIAM BROWN

Advent's waiting deepens.

First winter storms have turned the mechanized sounds of harvest abruptly into quiet. Early sunsets spread purples across the sky behind the barren trees. Night descends cold and clear.

Nature has begun its work of changing seasons in our human bones. Be still, it says, it is time to go slow and be attentive.

It takes some deliberateness on our part to enter into winter's special holiness. We have ways of keeping to our schedules despite "the conditions."

But we can let ourselves, at least sometimes, experience the call of winter. Leafless trees open up landscapes, revealing textures and shapes hidden at other times. A quiet woods offers the revelation of small sounds: tiny animals, cawing birds, shifting snow, and the distant voices of children.

Town street-lights lend special-effects as they catch the nighttime swirl of snow, and golden windows beckon us to warm gatherings around kitchen table or fire. We are wrapped in winter's holiness.

Sister Miriam Brown directs the Churches Center for Land and People at Sinsinawa Mound.

Ghost Territory

DENNIS BOYER

Wisconsin is the haunted heartland. Ghosts inhabit every acre of our lands and waters. Fecund spirits couple and multiply, blend traditions, and birth generation upon generation of stories.

Chasing these Wisconsin ghost stories makes a fellow aware of how our spirits arise from our relationship to the land. This, of course, is not an original flash of insight. The earliest paleo-Wisconsinites knew this right down in their marrow.

If you hanker to hear Wisconsin yarns, folktales, legends, and boisterous verbal bovine droppings, you'll best find them among those close to the land. If the tales are endangered as a species (and some insist they are), it is because the sources and settings of such tales are endangered too.

Up to now, Wisconsin has been good ghost habitat. Nearly every abandoned cheese factory and one room school boasts stories about spirit tenants. Just about all our waterfalls, islands, bluffs, and caves echo with tales of tribal mystery or pioneer suffering.

What happens to displaced ghosts? Where does sprawl push spirits? Does the arrival of the strip mall and the golden arches destroy the social and physical context needed for the transmission of folklore and the living of folklife?

Sources for ghost stories are a skittish breed and often dodge those questions. Those with a deep spiritual aura simply sniff that every inch of this land is sacred. Those haunted by politics and paranoia whisper about ghost mutations occasioned by land abuse (the trend, they say, turning benevolent spirits into malevolent forces). Those in the circle of wizards, shapeshifters, tricksters and redneck shamans see it as the black magic of pro-growth forces and work tirelessly on an antidote.

It is difficult to discuss these notions of spirit of place and sacredness of place within the modern political vocabulary. On the one hand, political leverage for preservation is accrued through emphasizing recreational value. On the other hand, an irksome subset of ecoactivists place their human fellows in the company of parasitic organisms.

Speak of the sacred, listeners nervously anticipate an evangelical pitch and worry over separation of church and state issues. Talk of spirits, those in earshot will swiftly retreat to the comfort of science. Few pause to ask whether we can truly protect the land, or at least use it prudently and respectfully, without a sense of awe and mystery about the Creation.

One of my recurrent folklore sources (and a redneck shaman mentor) has his own angle on this problem of secular hypersensitivity and the absence of the sacred from our political vocabulary.

"Doesn't matter," he says, "if you attend church, fly fish, hike, garden, or homebrew to find your way.

"What matters is that the land is our shared connection to the Great Mystery. Those with a land connection have a common ground for discussion. Doesn't matter if you chalk it up to God, Gaia, the Great Pumpkin, or in my case, the pondering of all such possibilities on a lakeside dock at dusk, with the benefit of Camel straights and Leinenkugels.

"Nevermind that we use different languages to chart our map. Doesn't matter a whit that one person might use ecclesiastical terms, when the next guy slobbers pop culture's warm fuzzies, and another upright knuckledragger just musters a satisfied grunt. If the vista makes all three jaws drop, or if an ugly scar on the land pains all three hearts, then there's a bond in spirit.

"Those who do not have this land connection do not know what the rest of us are talking about. To them, it's just choices. Strip mall or bike path. Winners and losers. They see land as a dead thing. Maybe they're dead inside too. Unfortunately, they're heavily clustered in the economic and political institutions where they can do the most harm.

"How do you get the likes of them to listen to a ghost story and accept that our land ghosts are guardian angels and patron saints of place? They don't understand how the stories tell us about troubles in the land.

"Cranky individualists talk of evil spirits set loose by federal agricultural policy. Hill farmers report on the demon of multiflora rose conjured up by wicked extension sorcerers. Naturalists complain about exotic vegetative poltergeists unleashed by landscapers and mindless prettifiers of all stripes.

"We're not just talking metaphors. Those wedded to the land feel the impact of land misuse. It doesn't matter whether the underlying human conduct is callous exploitation, boneheaded negligence, well-intentioned bumbling, or the best current and soon-to-be-debunked theory. They feel the disturbance in the energy and, yes, the spirit of the place.

"You gotta listen to those stooped old ladies, wizened bachelor farmers, dowsers, and woods hermits. They know ghosts real personal. They talk to the spirits and learn the lessons of love and cruelty that the land has to teach.

"When they tell you not to mess with a clump of woods or chunk of meadow, they're just not messing with your mind and your wallet. Nope, they're protecting your soul."

Dennis Boyer is a writer of folklore and fiction. He is the author of Driftless Spirits: Ghosts of Southwest Wisconsin *and other books.*

[1] Peter Berg and Raymond Dasmann. "Reinhabiting California," in Peter Berg, ed. Reinhabiting a Separate Country. San Francisco, CA: Planet Drum Foundation, pp. 217-220, quote from page 218.